Artwork:
Kelli Berens, Design
Laila Wright, Lettering
Supervised by Jack Britton, Art Instructor

I

# Acknowledgements

I would like to thank my family and friends for their support; for Eric Vanstrom for his graphic artwork; Renee Holmes for her encouragement; and especially my husband, Clark, for being such a good cook and a supporter of this project.

Order blanks are included in back of book
for your convenience.

First Printing - February 1995
Second Printing - August 1995

ISBN 09644995-0-9
Copyright 1995

# What's For Dinner?

This is more than a cookbook -- it is a simple 12-week meal planner designed for busy people on-the-go!

At the beginning of the book is an Inventory Checklist for you to write in commonly needed weekly items or non-food items. Bright color-coded menu dividers indicate each week's menu with the matching grocery list on the back.

The items on the grocery lists are categorized by departments, a parenthesis ( ) means the items may already be in your food supply from a previous week, and as asterisk* means you can choose between two items. The meat proportions are for 3 to 4 ounces per person.

After each week's menu ar the recipes for the week -- usually with a meat, vegetable, and a fruit each day. Following the fruit recipe is the preparation directions for the next day such as thawing meat, chilling fruit, or making a salad. If you have your own favorite recipe, it can be stapled on the recipe not page at the end of the week. Day 7 is cook's choice.

The daily menus are colorful and nutritious. Usually Day 1 is considered a Sunday meal because it may be more expensive or may take longer preparation time; such as steak, pork chops, roasts, turkey, lasagna, and spaghetti. Many of the meals have just a few ingredients and even use some simple convenience food directions. DThe directions are written in easy to ready numerical steps.

In the back of the book is an index of the types of dishes included. The purpose of this meal planner is to provide a variety of dishes and to help in the planning and fixing of meals. Enjoy!

*Trisha*

P.S. An order form is provided in the back, as well as a questionnaire. It would be helpful if you would include any changes, corrections or ways to improve this cookbook.

# Materials and Equipment

**Utensils Needed:**
Measuring spoons
Measuring cups
Liquid 2-cup measurer
Pint jar with lid
Meat fork
Set of dishes (8-12)
Set of soup bowls (8-12)
Sugar bowl
Salt and pepper shakers
Set of silverware (8-12)
Set of water glasses (8-12)
Set of orange juice glasses
   (8-12)
Set of plastic serving bowls
   (small, medium, large)
Set of glass microwave/
   baking dishes
Serving plate
Two casserole dishes with
   lids
3-quart Corning Ware dish
Meat container (for
   marinating)
Glass pizza plate
7x9-inch baking dish
7x11-inch baking dish
9x9-inch baking dish
4 to 12 individual pudding
   dishes

Corning Ware pie dish
Shredder
Plastic spatula
Metal spatula
Plastic scraper
Serving spoons with and
   without holes
Cutting board
Vegetable scraper
Cheese slicer
Ice cream scoop
Heavy wooden spoon
Sharp knives
Steak knives
Paring knife
Serrated knife
Gravy ladle
Soup ladle
Basting brush & syringe
Extra large slotted stirring
   spoon
Long-handled tongs

**Electric Appliances:**
Toaster
Mixer
Blender
Slow cooker
Electric skillet
*Small portable gas grill

# Materials and Equipment

**Pans:**

*Preferably stainless steel*
Two 5-quart pans with lids
Large covered saucepan
    (2 qt.)
Medium covered saucepan
    (1 1/2 qt.)
Small covered saucepan
    (1 qt.)
8-inch Teflon-coated skillet
10-inch skillet with lid
Splatter screen
Large stainless steel
    soup pot
9x13-inch cake pan with lid
9x13-inch glass cooking dish
9x15-inch pan
Cookie sheet, 10x15 inches
11x14-inch pan

Medium roaster pan
Turkey roasting pan
Muffin pan
Two 5x9-inch loaf pans
Pie pan
Broiler pan

**Non-food Items:**
Paper towels
Toothpicks
Scouring pads
Plastic wrap
Aluminum foil
Muffin baking papers
Zip-lock bags
Sandwich bags
Trash bags
Wastebaskets

# Our Standard Abbreviations

| | | | | | |
|---|---|---|---|---|---|
| **tsp.** | - | teaspoon | **sm.** | - | small |
| **T.** | - | tablespoon | **med.** | - | medium |
| **c.** | - | cup | **lg.** | - | large |
| **oz.** | - | ounce or ounces | **pt.** | - | pint |
| **lb.** | - | pound or pounds | **qt.** | - | quart |
| **sq.** | - | square | **pk.** | - | peck |
| **doz.** | - | dozen | **bu.** | - | bushel |
| **ctn.** | - | carton or container | **env.** | - | envelope(s) |
| **pkg.** | - | package(s) | **pkt.** | - | packet(s) |
| **btl.** | - | bottle | **mg** | - | milligram(s) |
| **approx.** | - | approximately | **g** | - | gram(s) |
| **temp.** | - | temperature | | | |

# Equivalent Measurements

| | | | | |
|---|---|---|---|---|
| 3 tsp. | ...... | 1 Tbsp. | 12 Tbsp. ...... | 3/4 cup |
| 4 Tbsp. | ...... | 1/4 cup | 16 Tbsp. ...... | 1 cup |
| 5 1/3 Tbsp. | ...... | 1/3 cup | 1/2 cup ...... | 1 gill |
| 8 Tbsp. | ...... | 1/2 cup | 2 cups ...... | 1 pt. |
| 10 2/3 Tbsp. | ...... | 2/3 cup | | |

(For liquid and dry measurements use standard measuring
spoons and cups. All measurements are level.)

# Terms Used in Recipes

**Bake** - To cook covered or uncovered in an oven or oven-type appliance. For meats cooked uncovered, it's called roasting.

**Baste** - To moisten foods during cooking with pan drippings or special sauce to add flavor and prevent drying.

**Beat** - To make mixture smooth by adding air with a brisk whipping or stirring motion using spoon or electric mixer.

**Blend** - To thoroughly mix two or more ingredients until smooth and uniform.

**Boil** - To cook in liquid at boiling temperature (212° at sea level) where bubbles rise to the surface and break. For a full rolling boil, bubbles form rapidly throughout the mixture.

**Broil** - To cook by direct heat, usually in broiler or over coals.

**Brown** - Use a little oil or browning sauce and fry or bake until brown, then turn over and darken on the other side without burning.

**Chill** - To place in refrigerator to reduce temperature.

**Chop** - To cut into pieces about the size of peas with knife, chopper, or blender.

**Cool** - To remove from heat and let stand at room temperature.

**Cream** - To beat with spoon or electric mixer until mixture is soft and smooth. When applied to blending shortening and sugar, mixture is beaten until light and fluffy.

**Cube** - To cut into a square or cube.

**Cut in** - To mix shortening with dry ingredients using pastry blender or knives.

**Defrost** - To thaw for a few hours or use the microwave "defrost" button.

**Dice** - To cut food in small cubes of uniform size and shape.

**Dissolve** - To disperse a dry substance in a liquid to form a solution.

**Drain** - Remove the liquid by pouring through a draining appliance or keep the lid slightly off to the side, while tipping pan or bowl upside down.

**Fold** - Overturn mixture without stirring or beating.

**Fried** - Cooked in a pan containing oil.

**Glaze** - A mixture applied to food which hardens or becomes firm and adds flavor and a glossy appearance.

**Grate** - To rub on a grater that separates the food into very fine particles.

**Marinate** - To allow food to stand in a liquid to tenderize or to add flavor.

**Mix** - To combine ingredients, usually by stirring, until evenly distributed.

**Preheat** - Warm the oven before beginning to bake.

**Purée** - Making a thick paste or liquid from vegetables.

**Roast** - To cook uncovered without water added, usually in an oven.

**Sauté** - To brown or cook in a small amount of hot shortening.

**Shred** - To cut or tear into pieces or using a shredder.

**Simmer** - To cook slowly in liquid at a temperature below boiling.

**Steam** - To cook with liquid in a covered pan under pressure for a few minutes, without boiling and vegetables remain bright colors and slightly crisp to eat.

**Stewed** - To boil slowly or with simmering heat.

**Stir** - To mix ingredients with a circular motion until well blended or of uniform consistency.

**Toasted** - Browning on one or two sides in toaster or broiler.

**Toss** - To mix ingredients lightly.

**Whip** - To beat rapidly to incorporate air and produce expansion, as in heavy cream or egg whites.

# Guide for Broiling Meat

## Broiling Beef Steaks

| Thickness of cut | Approximate Total Cooking Time | | |
|---|---|---|---|
| | **Rare** | **Medium** | **Well-done** |
| 1-inch beef steaks | 8-10 min. | 12-14 min. | 18-20 min. |
| 1 1/2-inch beef steaks | 14-16 min. | 18-20 min. | 25-30 min. |
| 2-inch beef steaks | 20-25 min. | 30-35 min. | 40-45 min. |

**Special Instructions for Beef Steaks:** Choose beef porter-house, T-bone, top loin, sirloin, or tenderloin steaks. Place steak on unheated rack in broiler pan. Broil 1- to 1 1/2-inch-thick steaks so surface of meat is 3 inches from heat. Broil thicker cuts 4 to 5 inches from heat. Broil on one side for about half the time indicated for desired doneness. Season. Turn with tongs; broil for remaining time. Season. To test for doneness, slit center and note inside color: red=rare; pink=medium; gray=well done.

## Broiling Ham, Pork and Lamb

| Thickness of cut | Approximate Total Cooking Time |
|---|---|
| 1-inch ham slice | 16-20 min. |
| 3/4- to 1-inch pork rib or loin chops | 20-25 min. |
| 1/2- to 3/4-inch pork shoulder steaks | 20-22 min. |
| 3/4-inch lamb rib or loin chops | 10-12 min. (medium) |
| 1-inch lamb rib or loin chops | 11-13 min. (medium) |
| 1 1/2-inch lamb rib or loin chops | 15-18 min. (medium) |

**Special Instructions for Ham, Pork and Lamb:** Place meat on unheated rack in broiler pan. Broil so surface of meat is 3 inches from heat (check range instruction booklet). Broil on one side of meat for about half of the time indicated. Season with salt and pepper (do not salt the ham). Turn and broil for remaining time suggested in chart or until desired doneness. Season again with salt and pepper.

## Broiling Other Meats

| Type of meat | Approximate Total Cooking Time |
|---|---|
| 1/4-inch hamburger (3 inches from heat) | 10 min. |
| Chicken halves (5-7 inches from heat) | 40 min. |

# MEAT ROASTING GUIDE

| Cut | Weight Pounds | Approx. Time (Hrs.) (325°) | Internal Temp. |
|---|---|---|---|
| **BEEF** | | | |
| Standing Rib Roast (10-inch ribs) | 4 | 1 3/4 | 140° (rare) |
| Allow 30 min. longer for 8-inch cut | | 2 | 160° (medium) |
| | | 2 1/2 | 170° (well done) |
| | 8 | 2 1/2 | 140° (rare) |
| | | 3 | 160° (medium) |
| | | 4 1/2 | 170° (well done) |
| Rolled Ribs | 4 | 2 | 140° (rare) |
| | | 2 1/2 | 160° (medium) |
| | | 3 | 170° (well done) |
| | 6 | 3 | 140° (rare) |
| | | 3 1/4 | 160° (medium) |
| | | 4 | 170° (well done) |
| Rolled Rump | 5 | 2 1/4 | 140° (rare) |
| | | 3 | 160° (medium) |
| | | 3 1/4 | 170° (well done) |
| Sirloin Tip | 3 | 1 1/2 | 140° (rare) |
| Roast only if high | | 2 | 160° (medium) |
| quality, otherwise braise | | 2 1/4 | 170° (well done) |
| **LAMB** | | | |
| Leg | 6 | 3 | 175° (medium) |
| | | 3 1/2 | 180° (well done) |
| | 8 | 4 | 175° (medium) |
| | | 4 1/2 | 180° (well done) |
| **VEAL** | | | |
| Leg (piece) | 5 | 2 1/2 - 3 | 170° (well done) |
| Shoulder | 6 | 3 1/2 | 170° (well done) |
| Rolled Shoulder | 3-5 | 3 - 3 1/2 | 170° (well done) |

# POULTRY ROASTING GUIDE

| Type of Poultry | Ready-To-Cook Weight | Oven Temp. | Approx. Total Roasting Time |
|---|---|---|---|
| **TURKEY** | 6-8 lbs. | 325° | 2 1/2 - 3 hrs. |
| | 8-12 lbs. | 325° | 3 - 3 1/2 hrs. |
| | 12-16 lbs. | 325° | 3 1/2 - 4 hrs. |
| | 16-20 lbs. | 325° | 4 - 4 1/2 hrs. |
| | 20-24 lbs. | 325° | 5-6 hrs. |
| **CHICKEN** | 2 - 2 1/2 lbs. | 400° | 1 - 1 1/2 hrs. |
| (Unstuffed) | 2 1/2 - 4 lbs. | 400° | 1 1/2 - 2 1/2 hrs. |
| | 4-8 lbs. | 325° | 3-5 hrs. |
| **DUCK** | 3-5 lbs. | 325° | 2 1/2 - 3 hrs. |
| (Unstuffed) | | | |

NOTE: Small chickens are roasted at 400° so that they brown well in the short cooking time. They may also be done at 325° but will take longer and will not be as brown. Increase cooking time 15 to 20 minutes for stuffed chicken and duck.

# Table of Contents



IX

*(Continued)*

*(Continued)*

*(Continued)*

# Table of Contents



# Inventory Checklist
## (Each Week Check)

**<u>Bakery</u>**
Bread

**<u>Baking Goods</u>**
Salt, pepper, flour,
sugar, oil, cornstarch,
mayonnaise

**<u>Dairy</u>**
Milk, butter, eggs

**<u>Produce</u>**
Onions
Fresh in-season
    fruits & vegetables

**<u>Cereal</u>**
Chips, snacks, peanut butter

**<u>Drinks</u>**
Coffee, soda pop, orange juice

**<u>Cleansers</u>**
Dust spray, bar & dish soap,
bleach, detergent,
toothpaste, shampoo

**<u>Paper Products</u>**
Bathroom tissue, bags,
plastic/foil wrap, napkins,
paper towels, tissues

# Week One

**Day 1** Fried Chicken  
Mashed Potatoes  
Gravy  
Corn  
Grapes

**Day 2** Broccoli-Stuffed Potatoes  
Breaded Fish Sandwiches  
Apple-Snickers Dessert

**Day 3** Chili/Soup  
Peanut Butter Sandwiches  
Relishes  
Bananas

**Day 4** Beef Stew  
Cut Green Beans  
Pears

**Day 5** Chili Dogs  
Watergate Salad

**Day 6** Stuffed Chicken Breasts  
Franciscan Vegetables  
Wild Rice  
Orange Slices

**Week 1:** Chicken, Fish Sandwich, Chili, Beef Stew, Chili Dogs, Stuffed Chicken Breasts

## Bakery
bread, hot dog buns
sesame seed buns
soda crackers
fine, dry bread crumbs

## Baking Goods
salt, pepper, sugar, flour,
cornstarch, oil, sage,
chili powder, paprika
cumin powder, parsley
1 pkg. chili seasoning
3 oz. instant pistachio pudding
3 oz. instant vanilla pudding
8 oz. mini marshmallows

## Frozen Foods
10 oz. kernel corn
10-16 oz. broccoli
*16 oz. stew vegetables
16 oz. Franciscan vegetables
16 oz. whipped topping
breaded fish squares

## Dairy
milk, eggs, butter,
16 oz. Velveeta cheese
16 oz. Cheddar cheese
mozzarella cheese slices
8 oz. Parmesan cheese

## Packaged Goods
lemon juice, mayonnaise
Worchestershire sauce,
tartar sauce, chili beans
16 oz. cut green beans
28 oz. puréed tomatoes
46 oz. tomato juice
26 oz. peaches
20 oz. pears
20 oz. crushed pineapple
chicken boullion
env. dry onion soup
box chicken coating
box instant wild rice
peanut butter
lg. Snickers candy bar

## Meat
pkg. hot dogs
4-6 lb. chicken, cut
4-6 chicken breasts
   (skinned, de-boned)
3 lb. ground beef
2 lb. stew meat
1/2 lb. thin ham slices

## Produce
5 lb. potatoes
tomatoes, radish, carrots,
celery, onion, lettuce,
2 Granny Smith apples, grapes,
6 bananas, 3 oranges

## Paper
paper towels

# Day 1

1. Thaw chicken within its bag.
2. Place in cold water.
3. Refrigerate when thawed.

## Fried Chicken

**(1/4 lb. chicken per person)**

**4 to 6 lb. fryer chicken,
    cut up**

**3 T. vegetable oil
1 box chicken coating**

1. Skin if desired.
2. Follow directions for chicken coating.
3. Fry in electric skillet with oil, use lid.
4. Fry each side at 350° for 15 to 20 minutes until crisp and well done.

## Mashed Potatoes

**8 potatoes, peeled & cut
    in large chunks**

**4 T. oleo
1/4 c. milk**

1. Use 5-quart pan and cover potatoes with water; boil.
2. Save water from drained potatoes.
3. Add butter; beat with mixer. Add hot, not boiling, milk, a little at a time; salt and pepper.
4. Beat until smooth.

## Corn

**1 pkg. frozen OR can of corn**

1. Cover.
2. Microwave for 7 minutes, or heat on stove.

# Gravy

**3 c. potato water**  **3 tsp. chicken bouillon**

**THICKENING:**
**3 T. cornstarch/or flour**  **1/2 c. potato water**

1. Remove fried chicken from pan.
2. Drain grease. Save chicken drippings.
3. Add 3 cups potato water and chicken bouillon.
4. Use chicken drippings.
5. Add chicken drippings to water in medium pan and heat on stove (add chicken bouillon).
6. Stir cornstarch and 1/2 cup water.
7. Slowly add thickening to simmering skillet.
8. Stir constantly until desired thickness.
        OR
Use equal amounts of flour and liquid (3 to 4 tablespoons each) and place in pint jar and cover. Shake a few minutes, until smooth.
(For quick thickener for gravy, add some instant potatoes.)


# Grapes


***Hints for Potatoes***

*1. Shape mashed potatoes into a long roll; wrap in plastic wrap and refrigerate. The next day, slice and fry patties in butter.*

*A slice of cheese may be sandwiched between two thin potato slices and fried.*


*2. Combine mashed potatoes with chopped chives and put into cupcake liners. Top with grated cheese and broil until cheese melts.*

# Day 2

## Broccoli-Stuffed Potatoes

**6 lg. potatoes, cleaned**
**10 oz. frozen broccoli**

**6 cheese slices (Velveeta)**

1. Pierce potatoes with fork.
2. Place in microwave between 2 paper towels.
3. Cook 5 minutes FULL POWER. Turn potatoes over.
4. Cook 4 minutes FULL POWER.
5. Meanwhile: cook broccoli in small covered saucepan for 7 minutes with 1/4 cup water.
6. Take out potatoes, place on plate and slit with knife.
7. Add butter and top with cooked broccoli. Salt and pepper to taste.
8. Top with cheese and microwave for 1 minute.

## Breaded Fish Sandwiches

**6 pieces frozen breaded**
**   fish squares**

**Sesame seed buns**
**Tartar sauce**

1. Follow directions on package.

## Apple-Snickers Dessert

**1 (3 oz.) pkg. instant**
**   vanilla pudding**
**1/4 c. milk**

**8 oz. non-dairy whipped topping**
**2 Granny Smith apples**
**1 lg. Snickers bar**

1. Mix pudding, milk and whipped topping in serving dish.
2. Cut apples in pieces with peels left on.
3. Thinly slice Snickers bar and add.
4. Refrigerate.

**Prepare for Day 3:**
1. Thaw ground beef.

# Day 3

## Chili (Soup)

3 lb. ground beef

1 med. onion, diced

1 (46 oz.) can tomato juice*
1 (28 oz.) can tomatoes,
    puréed*
1 pkg. chili seasoning
1 T. chili powder

2 tsp. cumin powder
1 tsp. salt
1 tsp. pepper
1 T. Worcestershire sauce
1 T. lemon juice*

(*For thick chili: only 38 ounces tomato juice, 16 ounces puréed tomatoes
    and 2 teaspoons lemon juice.)

1 (10 oz.) can chili beans
    + crackers

1.  Brown meat and onion in 5-quart pan; drain.
2.  Use blender for tomatoes.
3.  Add the next 9 ingredients. Cook on medium heat until it bubbles;
    simmer.
4.  Before serving, microwave beans; add to chili.
5.  Can freeze leftovers.

## Relish Tray

6 carrots
4 celery stalks

1 pkg. radishes

## Peanut Butter Sandwich

Bread

Peanut butter

## Bananas

1.  Cut in half with skins on, or serve whole.

## Prepare for Day 4:
1.  Thaw chuck roast/stew meat.
2.  Cut up vegetables in evening or early morning. (Cover. Refrigerate until ready to cook.)
3.  Chill pears.

### *Hints for Cutting Up Onions*

*1. To avoid tears when peeling onions, peel them under cold water, or refrigerate before chopping.*

*2. Peel and quarter onions. Place in airtight bags and freeze. Use as needed, chopping with sharp knife while frozen.*

*3. Peel and quarter several onions. Add to blender with 1 cup of water. Pour through drainer and freeze in airtight bags or container, to be used as needed.*

# Day 4

## Beef Stew

2 lb. beef chuck/stew
    meat in 1 1/2" cubes
1 pkg. frozen stew
    vegetables <u>OR</u> 3
    carrots (cut up), 3
    potatoes (cut up),
    1/2 c. onion (diced)

1 env. dry onion soup mix
1 c. water
1 tsp. Worcestershire
    sauce
1 T. salt
1/2 tsp. pepper
1 tsp. paprika

1. Brown meat in pan on both sides.
2. Put all ingredients in a slow cooker.
3. Cook on LOW 10 to 12 hours, or on HIGH 5 to 6 hours.
4. Before serving, thicken with cornstarch or flour. Add a few drops of Kitchen Bouquet to darken gravy.

## Cut Green Beans

1. Heat in medium saucepan on stove.

## Chilled Pears

**Prepare for Day 5:**
1. Refrigerate pineapple.

***Hint for Stew***
*Remove fat from stews or soups by adding lettuce leaves to the pot - the fat will cling to them. Discard lettuce before serving.*
*OR*
*After refrigerating and the fat rises and hardens on the surface, scrape off.*

# Day 5

## Chili Dogs

1 pkg. hot dogs                 Chili (from Day 3)
1 pkg. hot dog buns

1.    **Optional:** Melt slice of cheese on top.

## Watergate Salad

1 (20 oz.) can crushed        1 (3 oz.) box dry pistachio
    pineapple                      instant pudding
1 (16 oz.) ctn. non-dairy     1 (8 oz.) pkg. mini marsh-
    whipped topping             mallows

1.    Mix and refrigerate in medium bowl.

**Prepare for Day 6:**
1.    Thaw chicken breasts and refrigerate.

# Day 6

## Stuffed Chicken Breasts

4 to 6 chicken breast
   halves, skinned,
   deboned & tenderized
   at store
4 to 6 thin slices of ham

2 to 3 slices mozzarella
   cheese, halved
1 med. tomato, seeded &
   chopped
1/2 tsp. sage

COATING:
4 T. melted margarine
1 T. parsley flakes

2 T. Parmesan cheese, grated
1/3 c. fine, dry bread crumbs

1. Place 1 ham slice and 1/2 slice cheese on each cutlet.
2. Top with some tomato and dash of sage.
3. Tuck in sides, roll up and press to seal.
4. Combine crumbs. Parmesan cheese and parsley.
5. Dip chicken in butter, then roll in crumbs.
6. Bake in shallow dish at 350° for 40 to 45 minutes.

## Franciscan Blend Vegetables

16 oz. frozen Franciscan vegetables

1. Microwave in covered dish for 7 minutes.

## Wild Rice

1 box instant wild rice

1. Follow box directions.

## Oranges

1. Slice oranges and place 2 to 3 slices on each plate.

## Prepare for Week 2:

1.  Thaw ham.
2.  Make Pineapple Gelatin.

***Hints for Tomatoes***

*1. Cut them vertically and they "bleed" less.*

*2. Fresh tomatoes keep longer if stored with the stems down.*

*3. Sunlight doesn't ripen  tomatoes.*
*Try placing them near a warm spot such as the stove or dishwasher where they can get a little heat.*
*Try placing tomatoes in a paper sack and close tightly, or cover with newspapers away from sunlight.*

# Notes & Recipes

# Week Two

**Day 1** Baked/Grilled Ham
Fried Potatoes
Tomato Slices
Pineapple Gelatin

**Day 2** Rigatoni in Red Sauce
Steamed Broccoli
Garlic Bread

**Day 3** Homemade Vegetable Beef Soup
Cherry Squares

**Day 4** Scalloped Potatoes and Ham
Peas and Carrots
Fruit Cocktail

**Day 5** Crabmeat Salad
Cantaloupe

**Day 6** Spaghetti
Marinated Vegetables
Garlic Bread

**Week 2:** Ham, Rigatoni, Beef Soup, Scalloped Potatoes and Ham, Crabmeat Salad, Spaghetti

### Bakery
garlic bread

### Baking Goods
(sugar) (flour), baking powder,
garlic powder, Mrs. Dash,
vanilla, Cajun seasoning,
Italian seasoning, cloves,
oregano
3 oz. lemon gelatin
cherry pie filling

### Packaged Goods
ketchup, mustard, mayonnaise
pickle slices, Heinz 57
honey, Italian dressing
dry Italian salad dressing
Kitchen Bouquet sauce
46 oz. tomato juice
12 oz. tomato paste
26 oz. tomatoes
17 oz. fruit cocktail
20 oz. pineapple slices
20 oz. pineapple chunks
4 oz. can crabmeat
10 oz. potato soup
10 oz. cream of celery soup
env. dry onion soup
11 oz. pkg. barley
8 oz. wide egg noodles
box rigatoni noodles/or
    mostaccioli
pkg. spaghett noodles

### Dairy
milk, eggs, butter
shredded mozzarella

### Frozen Foods
*or frozen melon balls
8 oz. salad shrimp
16 oz. imitation crabmeat

### Meat
1 lb. arm roast
2 lb. ground beef
1 lb.ground Italian sausage
4 lb. buffet ham, pre-cooked

### Produce
5 lb. potatoes,
4 onions, celery
carrots, 2 broccoli
cauliflower
3 tomatoes, lettuce
*OR cantaloupe and honeydew

### Other
toothpicks

# Day 1

## Baked/Grilled Ham

4 T. Heinz 57
2 T. honey
4 lb. precooked buffet
ham

3 pineapple slices
7 to 15 cloves
Toothpicks

1. Put ham in roaster pan.
2. Remove both plastic and paper wrappings.
3. Mix Heinz 57 and honey; spread on ham.
4. Pierce ham with rows of cloves.
5. Use toothpicks to place pineapple slices on top.
6. Cover. Bake at 375° for 1 hour <u>or</u> grill in a 9x13-inch pan on low heat for 1 hour.
7. Continually baste.
8. Save remaining ham for Day 4.

## Fried Potatoes

6 potatoes, cleaned &
   sliced
2 T. oil

Salt & pepper
Cajun seasoning

1. Use electric skillet or fry pan with splatter screen.
2. Put oil in pan and fry on medium heat, turning only until brown.
3. Shake seasonings on both sides.

## Sliced Tomatoes

## Chilled Pineapple Gelatin

3 oz. lemon gelatin

Pineapple chunks

1. Follow gelatin package directions.
2. Cut up pineapple into chunks and add to gelatin mix, <u>or</u> use chilled pineapple chunks.

## Prepare for Day 2:
1.   Thaw ground beef and Italian sausage.
2.   Prepare meat sauce.

# Day 2

## Rigatoni in Red Sauce

**MEAT:**
1 lb. ground beef
1/2 lb. Italian sausage, ground

1/2 onion, diced
1 tsp. salt
1/2 tsp. pepper

**SAUCE:**
12 oz. tomato paste
46 oz. tomato juice
1 T. Italian seasoning

1 tsp. oregano
1 tsp. garlic powder
1 tsp. salt

**RIGATONI NOODLES:**
6 to 8 oz. rigatoni/or
   mostaccioli

1 pkg. Mozzarella cheese,
   shredded

1. Brown meat and onions in 5-quart pan.
2. Simmer sauce in separate 5-quart pan 1/2 to 1 hour.
3. Add sauce and meat to one pan.
4. Clean pan, boil water and cook noodles until tender.
5. Drain noodles and rinse with cold water.
6. Roaster Pan: Layer noodles, then 1/2 of pasta sauce.
7. Save 1/2 pasta sauce for Day 6.
8. Cover.
9. Bake at 375° for 30 minutes.
10. Add cheese and melt.

## Steamed Broccoli

**Bunch of broccoli, cut up**

1. Heat in large covered saucepan in 1/2 cup water for 15 minutes.

## Garlic Bread

**1 loaf garlic bread**
**1/2 c. soft butter**

**1 T. garlic powder**

1. Mix garlic powder with soft butter.
2. Spread on slices of bread.
3. Broil carefully for a few minutes.

## Prepare for Day 3:

1. Thaw beef roast.
2. **Notice:** Morning cooking in crock-pot!
3. Can cut up carrots and onions (cover and refrigerate vegetables).

# Day 3

## Homemade Vegetable Soup
**(See Day 2 for directions!)**

| | |
|---|---|
| 1 lb. beef roast | 1 sm. onion, diced |
| 1 T. browning & seasoning sauce (Kitchen Bouquet) | 1/4 c. barley |
| | 1 env. dry onion soup |
| 3 carrots, diced | 1 (26 oz.) can tomatoes |
| 3 potatoes, diced | Salt & pepper to taste |
| 8 c. water | 8 oz. wide egg noodles |

1. Use crock-pot in morning!
2. Brown roast in 5-quart pan with 1 tablespoon oil.
3. Add browning sauce.
4. Place in crock-pot.
5. Use food processor for tomatoes if family doesn't like chunks of tomatoes.
6. Add other ingredients.
7. Cook on MEDIUM all day.

**Noodles:**
8. Boil water in large saucepan.
9. Add noodles and boil 15 minutes; drain.
10. Add to soup 30 to 60 minutes before serving.

# Cherry Squares

Blend:
**2 oleo sticks, soft**
**1 3/4 c. sugar**

**1 tsp. vanilla**

Add:
**4 beaten eggs**

Mix.

**DRY INGREDIENTS:**
**3 c. flour**

**1 1/2 tsp. baking powder**
**1 1/2 tsp. salt**

**Cherry pie filling**

1. Combine dry ingredients in small bowl.
2. Use hand blender for other ingredients.
3. Mix together for batter.
4. Save 1 cup batter for later.
5. Spread batter in greased 11x27-inch pan.
6. Spread cherry pie filling on top.
7. Spoon islands of extra 1 cup of batter on top.
8. Bake at 350° for 30 minutes.

## Prepare for Day 4:

1. Boil 6 potatoes with skins on in 5-quart pan of water for 25 minutes.
2. Drain, cool, and refrigerate.
3. Chill fruit cocktail.

# Day 4

## Scalloped Potatoes and Ham

**Cooked ham, cubed**
**6 non-peeled potatoes**
**1 med. onion, diced**

**SAUCE:**
**3 T. flour**

**1 (10 oz.) can potato soup**
**1 (10 oz.) can cream of**
   **celery soup**

**3 c. milk**
**Salt & pepper**

1.   Cube cooked ham from Day 1.
2.   Peel cooked and cooled potatoes; slice thinly.
3.   Add onion, salt and pepper.
4.   In medium bowl, stir soups with flour.
5.   Add milk; stir. Add to meat and cover.
6.   Microwave on LOW heat 3 minutes; stir.
7.   Cook on FULL POWER 5 minutes; stir.
8.   Heat thoroughly <u>or</u> cover and bake at 350° for 45 minutes.

## Peas and Carrots

**10 to 16 oz. frozen mixed**
   **vegetables**

1.   Heat on stove in covered saucepan for 5 to 7 minutes.

## Fruit Cocktail

**Prepare for Day 5:**
1.   Make Crabmeat Salad.

# Day 5

## Crabmeat Salad

16 oz. frozen imitation
    crabmeat
4 oz. frozen salad shrimp
1 (4 oz.) can crabmeat
1 1/2 c. mayonnaise
4 chopped celery

1 med. onion
Salt & pepper
Mrs. Dash
Lettuce leaves
3 tomatoes, wedged

1. Defrost frozen crabmeat and shrimp.
2. Combine all ingredients; chill 1 hour.
3. Serve on lettuce with tomato wedges.


## Cantaloupe and Honeydew

1. Slice melons and cut up in chunks.
2. Serve on plate beside crabmeat salad.
3. (If not in season, you can purchase frozen melon balls.)

## Prepare for Day 6:
1. Cut up and marinate vegetables.

# Day 6

## Spaghetti

**16 oz. spaghetti noodles**

1. Heat remaining Rigatoni sauce from Day 2.
2. In 5-quart pan, boil water and add spaghetti noodles.
3. Stir occasionally and cook until tender (about 20 minutes).
4. Drain.
5. Add cold water to remove paste; drain.
6. Add hot water to warm.
7. Drain and serve immediately.
8. Top with Rigatoni sauce.

## Garlic Bread

## Marinated Vegetables

**Cauliflower, bite-size**
**Broccoli, bite-size**
**1/2 onion, diced**
**3 carrots, diced**

**1 pkg. dry Italian salad**
    **dressing**
**1/2 c. Italian dressing**
**1 tsp. oregano**
**1 tsp. garlic powder**

1. Combine all ingredients in medium bowl.
2. Chill.

### Prepare for Week 3:
1. Defrost steak.
2. Marinate in covered plastic container.
3. Make coleslaw.
4. Make crust for sweet pizza.

# Notes & Recipes

# Week Three

**Day 1**  Beef Steak
Baked Potato
Sweet Pizza

**Day 2**  Shrimp Basket
Coleslaw
French Fries
Apple Wedges

**Day 3**  Homemade Chicken Noodle Soup
Strawberry Gelatin with Bananas

**Day 4**  Beef Oriental Stir-Fry

**Day 5**  Pizza Ham Sandwiches
Cold Pasta Salad
Grapes

**Day 6**  Chicken Casserole
Mashed Potatoes
Kernel Corn with Red Peppers
Orange Slices

## **Week 3:** Steak, Shrimp, Chicken Noodle Soup, Beef Stir-Fry, Pizza Sandwich, Chicken Casserole

**Bakery**
hamburger buns

**Baking Goods**
(oil, salt, pepper, sugar)
(cornstarch, oregano)
(garlic, Mrs. Dash)
sweet basil
*red food coloring
3 oz. strawberry gelatin

**Packaged Goods**
(mayonnaise) vinegar
Sauces: soy, shrimp, and
  teriyaki
8 oz. pizza sauce
pitted ripe olives
6 oz. jar jalapeños
17 oz. sliced peaches
14 oz. can chicken broth
32 oz. chicken broth
box of quick white rice
box of instant potatoes
16 oz. thin spaghetti

**Dairy**
(milk, eggs) butter
3 oz. cream cheese
3 oz. sour cream
10 oz. sugar cookie tube
sliced Swiss cheese

**Frozen Foods**
16 oz. oriental vegetables
12 oz. corn with red pepper
16 oz. French fries
16-20 oz. breaded shrimp
12 oz. egg noodles
8 oz. whipped topping
10 oz. Brussels sprouts

**Meat**
1 1/2 lb. shaved ham
1 1/2 lb. round steak
4-6 sirloin steaks
3-5 lb. whole chicken

**Produce**
5 lb. potatoes, 2 onions
celery, carrots
shredded cabbage and
  carrots
cabbage, 5 tomatoes
3 green peppers
3 oranges
6 bananas, 3 apples, grapes
strawberries
*or strawberry glaze

**Paper**
paper towels

# Day 1

## Beef Steak

**(See Week 2, Day 6 directions)**

**MEAT:**

**4 to 6 sirloin steaks**          **1/4 c. teriyaki sauce**

1.   Marinate steak in sauce overnight <u>or</u> for 1 hour.
2.   Grill steaks (or broil).

## Baked Potato

**4 to 6 potatoes**          **3 oz. sour cream**

1.   Place between paper towels in microwave.
2.   Cook 4 minutes.
3.   Turn over.
4.   Cook 4 minutes.

## Brussels Sprouts

**1 pkg. Brussels sprouts**          **1 T. vinegar**
**1/4 c. water**

1.   Simmer in covered saucepan for 20 minutes.
2.   Salt and pepper to taste.

# Sweet Pizza

**10 oz. sugar cookie dough**
**3 oz. cream cheese**
**4 bananas, sliced**
**17 oz. sliced peaches**
**Strawberries**

**Strawberry glaze**
  **(purchased)***
**8 oz. non-dairy whipped**
  **topping**
**Red food coloring**

**Crust:**
1.  Spread 1/2 of cookie dough in a 9x7-inch dish.
2.  Bake at 350° for 7 to 9 minutes.
3.  Cool.

***Glaze:** (Can make own.)
4.  Boil 3/4 cup water with 3/4 cup sugar until dissolved.
5.  Mix 2 tablespoons cornstarch with 1/4 cup water in cup.
6.  Mix into sugar water.
7.  Add 8 drops red food coloring.
8.  Stir until thick.
9.  Refrigerate while layering pizza.

10.  Spread cream cheese on cooled crust.
11.  Place bananas on cream cheese layer.
12.  Place peaches on banana layer, covering all bananas.
13.  Top with cooled or purchased glaze.
14.  Refrigerate.
15.  Top each serving with whipped topping.

# Prepare for Day 2:
1.  Make Coleslaw.

# Prepare for Day 3:
1.  Thaw chicken within its bag in cold water.
2.  Refrigerate when thawed.

# Day 2

## Shrimp Basket

**1 to 2 boxes frozen,
  prepared popcorn shrimp**

**Shrimp sauce**

1. Follow box directions.

## Coleslaw

**1/2 head cabbage, shredded
  <u>OR</u> 1 pkg. shredded
  cabbage & carrots
4 carrots, shredded**

**1/2 onion, diced
1 tsp. salt
1/8 tsp. pepper**

**SAUCE:
1 c. mayonnaise
1/2 c. sugar**

**1/4 c. vinegar
Salt & pepper**

1. Shred cabbage and carrots, or may choose to use pre-packaged shredded cabbage and carrots.
2. Add onion.
3. Mix sauce separately. Then add in medium bowl.
4. Chill.

## French Fries

1. Follow package directions.

## Apple Wedges

**3 apples, cored & sliced**

# Prepare for Day 3:

**Salad**

    1. Make red gelatin with bananas.

**Poultry**

    1. Place chicken in roaster pan with 4 cups chicken broth, salt and pepper.
    2. Add diced carrots, celery and onion.
    3. Bake at 375° for 1 hour.
    4. Cool chicken slightly.
    5. Take off skin and debone.
    6. Cube 2 cups chicken; freeze remainder.
    7. Place all in a sealed container and refrigerate.

# Day 3

## Homemade Chicken Noodle Soup
**(See directions: Day 2)**

**Chicken (fryer)**
**6 carrots, diced**
**4 celery stalks, diced**
**1 med. onion, diced**

**4 c. chicken broth**
**2 tsp. salt & pepper**
**2 tsp. Mrs. Dash**

**Egg Noodles:**
**1 pkg. frozen**

**1 T. salt**

1. Chicken and vegetables should be cooked Day 2!
2. Heat chicken and vegetables in large pot.
3. Add 4 cups water.

**Noodles:**
3. In separate 5-quart pan, boil noodles in salted water.
4. Add frozen noodles and cook until tender to eat.
5. Drain.
6. Heat chicken and vegetables thoroughly on medium heat.
7. Add noodles to chicken mixture.
8. Save extra for Day 6 Chicken Casserole.

## Strawberry Gelatin with Bananas

**3 oz. strawberry gelatin**
**2 bananas**

**Whipped topping**

1. Prepare gelatin according to box directions.
2. Add sliced bananas, making sure gelatin covers them.
3. Top each serving with whipped topping.

## Prepare for Day 5:
1. Thaw steak and marinate in teriyaki sauce.

# Day 4

## Beef Oriental Stir-Fry #1
**(See Day 4)**

2 T. cooking oil
1 1/2 lb. round steak,
    marinated
2 c. quick white rice
2 c. water

16 oz. frozen Oriental
    vegetables <u>OR</u> 1/2 head
    cabbage, 1/2 med. onion
    (chopped), 2 celery
    stalks (chopped), 1
    green pepper (chopped)

**SAUCE:**
2 T. water

2 T. soy sauce
1 T. cornstarch

1. Add oil to fry pan and brown meat.
2. Remove meat from pan.
3. Quickly fry vegetables so partially cooked, but still bright color and crunchy.
4. Add meat to vegetables and warm.
5. Meanwhile, cook rice according to box directions for 4 to 6 people.

**Sauce:**
6. Add ingredients in a cup; stir.
7. Pour over stir-fry. Heat 2 minutes.
8. Serve immediately over dish of rice.

## Coleslaw (See Day 2)

## Red Gelatin Dessert (See Day 3)

## Prepare for Day 5:
1. Thaw sliced ham.
2. Make pasta salad.

# Day 5

## Cold Pasta Salad

5 tomatoes, diced
2 green peppers, diced
1 lg. onion, diced
15 oz. ripe olives, sliced
3 T. salad/olive oil
1 1/2 T. vinegar

5 to 6 jalapeños, diced
1 tsp. oregano
1 tsp. sweet basil
1 T. garlic powder
1 T. salt
Pepper

**1 pkg. pasta (very thin noodles--cook's choice)**

1. Combine all ingredients in medium bowl, <u>except</u> pasta noodles.
2. Chill.

3. Add noodles to boiling water.
4. Cook until tender (not chewy); drain.
5. Add cold water and drain again; cover.
6. Serve cold marinated vegetables over noodles.

## Pizza Ham Sandwiches

1 pkg. hamburger buns
1 1/2 lb. thin-sliced ham

1 (8 oz.) can pizza sauce
6 slices Swiss cheese

1. Butter 4 to 6 hamburger buns on each half.
2. Carefully broil until lightly browned.
3. Spoon 1 teaspoon pizza sauce on each half.
4. Add 2 slices ham to each half.
5. Broil again until warmed (2 minutes).
6. Top with slice of cheese per sandwich and melt.
7. Serve warmed sandwiches.

## Grapes

**Prepare for Week 4, Day 1:**
1. Thaw ground beef and sausage.

# Day 6

## Chicken Casserole
**(See Day 3)**

**Use Chicken Noodle Soup**          **14 oz. chicken broth**

**THICKENING SAUCE:**
**2 T. cornstarch**          **1/4 c. water**

1.    Microwave ingredients in covered casserole dish on FULL POWER for 4 minutes (may need to add broth).

**Sauce:**
2.    Stir cornstarch and water in cup, then add to casserole and stir.
3.    Cook 4 minutes; stir. Cook until warmed through.

## Mashed Potatoes

**1 box instant potatoes or make from scratch**

1.    Follow box directions for 4 to 6 servings.
2.    Serve chicken casserole over mashed potatoes.

## Corn with Red Peppers

**1 frozen pkg.**

1.    Cover.
2.    Microwave 7 minutes.

## Orange Slices

1.    Slice 3 oranges.

## Prepare for Week 4, Day 1:
1.    Prepare meat and sauce for lasagna.
2.    Chill pineapple chunks.

# Notes & Recipes

# *What Shall We Have for Dinner?*

## What to Serve with Meats

| | |
|---|---|
| ROAST PORK | Brown potatoes, applesauce or fruit salad<br>Sweet potatoes, sauerkraut<br>Mashed potatoes, celery or apple salad |
| PORK CHOPS | Scalloped potatoes, fried apple rings<br>Mashed potatoes, cabbage salad |
| BAKED HAM | Sweet potatoes, spinach<br>Rice, fried pineapple rings<br>Parsley potatoes, asparagus |
| COLD HAM | Baked beans, relish, egg rolls<br>Potato salad, dill pickles |
| BACON | Corn fritters, maple syrup |
| HAM STEAK | Buttered rice, glazed pineapple<br>Fried eggs, hash brown potatoes<br>Hominy, corn muffins, fried bananas |
| SAUSAGE | Fried apples, cornbread<br>Mashed potatoes, pickled peaches |
| VEAL CUTLET | Baked potato, tossed salad |
| LAMB CHOPS | Buttered parsley potatoes, succotash<br>Browned potatoes, spinach, peas |
| LAMB STEW | Dumplings, green salad |
| ROAST LAMB | Mashed potatoes, currant jelly |
| LIVER | Bacon, cornbread |
| HAMBURGER | Toasted buns, sweet onion rings<br>Potato salad, carrots |
| CORNED BEEF HASH | Poached eggs, green salad |
| MEAT LOAF | Baked potato, canned tomatoes<br>French fried potatoes, asparagus |
| FRANKFURTER | Sauerkraut, baked beans |
| CHIPPED BEEF | Baked potatoes, green salad |

# Week Four

**Day 1** Lasagna
Lettuce Salad
Garlic Bread
Pineapple and Bananas

**Day 2** BLT Sandwich (Bacon, Lettuce, Tomato)
Potato Salad
Apple Wedges

**Day 3** Grilled Chicken Breast
Cheesy Broccoli Bake
Cantaloupe

**Day 4** Ham and Cabbage Soup
Peach Dessert

**Day 5** Chicken Oriental Stir-Fry
(Ravioli for kids)
Rice
Orange Slices

**Day 6** Shrimp & Crabmeat Lettuce Salad
Ham and Cabbage Soup
Blueberry Muffins

**Week 4:** Lasagna, BLT, Chicken Breast, Ham and
Cabbage Soup, Chicken Stir-Fry, Shrimp Salad

### Bakery
(soda crackers)
bread, garlic bread

### Baking Goods
(sugar)
(flour, cinnamon, oil)
(garlic powder, vinegar)
(parsley flakes)
basil, fennel seeds
box blueberry muffins
muffin baking cups

### Packaged Goods
(soy sauce, mayonnaise)
(Italian dressing, pickles)
Ranch dressing
6 oz. tomato paste
16 oz. tomatoes
32 oz. peach slices
20 oz. pineapple chunks
10 oz. cream of mushroom soup
20 ravioli (for kids)
6 oz. water chestnuts
box instant white rice
box lasagna noodles

### Dairy
(butter) eggs
16 oz. Velveeta
16 oz. Cheez Whiz
Parmesan cheese
shredded mozzarella
8 oz. Ricotta/cottage cheese

### Frozen
20 oz. broccoli
16 oz. pea pods
8 oz. salad shrimp
16 oz. imitation crabmeat

### Meat
1/2 lb. ground beef
1/2 lb. ground Italian sausage
6 to 10 chicken breasts
2-3 lb. picnic ham
16 oz. bacon slices

### Produce
5 lb. red potatoes, 4 onions
carrots, lettuce,  6 tomatoes
cabbage, 2 bananas
3 apples, 3 oranges,
cantaloupe

# Day 1

## Lasagna

**MEAT:**
1/2 lb. Italian sausage
1/2 lb. ground beef

1/4 c. onion, diced
2 tsp. garlic powder

**COTTAGE CHEESE:**
8 oz. ricotta/cottage
   cheese

1 egg, beaten
1 T. parsley flakes
1/4 tsp. salt

**SAUCE:**
2 c. mashed tomatoes
6 oz. tomato paste
1/4 c. water
1 T. sugar

2 tsp. salt
2 tsp. parsley flakes
1 tsp. basil
1/4 tsp. fennel seeds
1/4 tsp. pepper

4 lasagna noodles
1 pkg. Mozzarella cheese

2 T. Parmesan cheese

1. Brown meat ingredients in 5-quart pan.
2. Meanwhile, cook sauce ingredients in 5-quart pan.
3. Drain browned meat and add cooked sauce. Cook on low to medium heat.
4. Wash 5-quart pan, add water and bring to a boil.
5. Cook 4 lasagna noodles until tender (not chewy).
6. Meanwhile, prepare cheese by adding all ingredients in small bowl.
7. Drain noodles. Add cold water, then drain again.
8. Use a 7x9-inch glass baking dish.
9. Add 1 1/2 cups meat sauce.
10. 2 noodles.
11. Spread 1/2 of cottage cheese
12. 1/2 package Mozzarella shredded cheese.
13. 1 tablespoon Parmesan cheese.
14. Repeat for second layer.
15. Cover with foil. Bake at 375° for 25 minutes.
16. Uncover. Bake 25 minutes.
17. Cool 15 minutes before serving.
18. Can freeze leftovers.

## Garlic Bread

# Lettuce Salad

1. Tear 1/2 head lettuce.
2. Add tomato wedges and chopped onion.
3. Serve with Italian dressing.

# Pineapple and Bananas

**20 oz. pineapple chunks**                     **2 bananas, sliced**

1. Mix both fruits in bowl and serve.

## Prepare for Day 2:
1. Boil 6 nonpeeled red potatoes in 5-quart pan of water for 25 minutes; drain. Refrigerate.
2. Peel and dice while still warm.
3. Marinate with 1/4 cup Italian dressing.

# Day 2

## Bacon, Lettuce and Tomato Sandwich (BLT)

**Bread slices**
**4 to 6 slices bacon, fried**
**Lettuce**
**2 to 3 tomatoes, sliced**

**Pickles & onion slices**
**4 to 6 slices Velveeta cheese**
**Butter**

1. Make toast and butter.
2. Broil or fry bacon until crisp.
3. Place cooked bacon on plate with paper towels.
4. Slice tomatoes.
5. Tear apart lettuce leaves.
6. Arrange layers of food between 2 slices of toast.
7. Cut diagonally.

## Potato Salad
**(See Day 1 for directions)**

**6 nonpeeled red potatoes**
**1 med. onion, diced**

**1/4 c. Italian dressing**
**6 eggs, boiled**

**SAUCE:**
**1 c. mayonnaise**
**1/2 c. sugar**

**1 T. mustard**
**1/4 c. vinegar**
**Salt & pepper**

1. Boil eggs for 20 minutes; cool in cold water and peel.
2. Use 3-quart bowl.
3. Dice or slice potatoes in large bowl.
4. Add diced onions and Italian dressing and chill.
5. Prepare sauce.
6. Mix with potatoes.
7. Refrigerate.

## Apple Wedges

## Prepare for Day 3:
1.  Marinate chicken with 1/4 cup Italian dressing.
2.  Cover and refrigerate.

## Prepare for Day 4:
1.  Thaw picnic ham.

## Prepare for Day 5:
1.  Thaw chicken breasts.
2.  Refrigerate when thawed.

# Day 3

## Grilled Chicken Breast
**(See Day 2 directions)**

**4 to 6 skinned chicken breasts**

**1/4 c. Italian dressing**
**2 T. cooking oil**

1. Marinate chicken in Italian dressing.
2. Add oil to electric skillet.
3. Fry marinated chicken breast about 10 minutes each side.

## Cheesy Broccoli Bake

**1 stick oleo**
**1 sm. onion, diced**
**8 oz. Cheez Whiz**
**10 oz. cream of mushroom soup or celery soup**

**1 c. instant rice, uncooked**
**10 oz. chopped broccoli, thawed**

1. Sauté oleo and butter.
2. Thaw broccoli and mix <u>all</u> ingredients together.
3. Place in uncovered casserole dish and bake at 350° for 30 minutes.

## Cantaloupe

1. Cut in half and remove seeds.
2. Thinly slice and remove outer skin.
3. Place 2 slices on each plate.

**Prepare for Day 4:**
1. Cook picnic ham; may use slow cooker in the morning.

# Day 4

## Ham and Cabbage Soup

1 sm. picnic ham
1/2 head cabbage, cut up
8 to 10 c. water
2 potatoes, cubed

1 onion, diced
4 carrots, diced
Salt & pepper

1.  Cook picnic ham in pot of water until it begins to fall apart from the bone.
2.  Remove ham from bone and add all ingredients and cook until vegetables are tender (45 minutes).
3.  Add all ingredients.
4.  OR use slow cooker. Cook on HIGH 5 or 6 hours or LOW 11 to 12 hours.
5.  Save remaining soup for Day 6.
    (If soupbone with less meat is used, use 3 tablespoons chicken-flavored base, or use 32 ounces chicken stock to replace some liquid.)

## Peach Dessert

**BATTER:**
1 c. flour
1 tsp. baking powder
1/2 c. sugar

1/2 c. milk
1 egg, beaten
2 T. butter

**FRUIT:**
32 oz. sliced peaches, drained

**TOPPING:**
1/2 c. sugar

2 tsp. cinnamon

1.  Use a 7x9-inch pan.
2.  Place fruit on bottom of pan.
3.  Sprinkle with mixed sugar and cinnamon.
4.  Pour batter on top.
5.  Bake at 375° for 25 minutes.

## Prepare for Day 5:

1.  Thaw chicken breasts.
2.  Marinate with teriyaki sauce.

# Day 5

## Chicken Oriental Stir-Fry
**(See Day 4 directions)**

2 to 4 chicken breasts, fried
1 onion, chopped
1 pkg. pea pods

1 (6 oz.) can water
  chestnuts
Salt & pepper
2 T. cooking oil

SAUCE:
2 T. water

2 T. soy sauce
1 T. cornstarch

**Meat:**
1.  Marinate and cube chicken.
2.  Use electric skillet; add oil.
3.  Fry cubed chicken quickly until browned on both sides.
4.  Add other vegetable ingredients and fry for 5 minutes.

**Sauce:**
5.  Mix in cup. Pour over chicken stir-fry.

6.  Place cooked rice on dish; top with stir-fry.
7
.  Shake more soy sauce on for extra seasoning.

## Instant White Rice
1.  Cook 4 to 6 servings rice per directions.

## Ravioli for the Kids
1.  Follow directions on the can.

## Orange Slices
1.  Slice and place 2 to 3 on each plate.

## Prepare for Day 6:

1.   Boil eggs; cool in water. Drain, shell, and refrigerate.

# Day 6

## Shrimp and Crabmeat Salad

**(See Day 5 directions)**

**Head of lettuce**
**1 (8 oz.) pkg. frozen salad shrimp**
**1 pkg. frozen crabmeat pieces**

**2 tomatoes, cut in wedges**
**3 hard-boiled eggs, sliced**
**Ranch dressing**
**Salad croutons**

1. Boil eggs for 15 minutes; drain.
2. Add cold water and shell immediately; refrigerate.
3. Thaw shrimp and crabmeat.
4. Tear lettuce in individual bowls.
5. Add thawed shrimp and crabmeat.
6. Top with tomato wedges, sliced eggs and croutons.
7. Serve with ranch dressing.

## Ham and Cabbage Soup

**(See Day 4)**

## Blueberry Muffins

**1 box blueberry muffin mix**

**1 pkg. baking cups**

1. Use box mix and bake according to directions.

**Prepare for Week 5:**
1. Thaw pork chops.
2. Chill peaches.

# Notes & Recipes

# Week Five

**Day 1** Grilled/Broiled Pork Chops
Steamed Cauliflower
Scalloped Corn
Peaches

**Day 2** Hot Beef Sandwiches
Instant Potatoes, Gravy
Three Bean Salad
Pears

**Day 3** Grilled Cheese Sandwich
Tomato Soup
Apple Wedges

**Day 4** French Dip Aus Jus
Spinach/Lettuce Salad
Mandarin Orange Salad

**Day 5** Porcupine Meatballs
Ramen Noodle Salad
Warmed Applesauce

**Day 6** Shrimp Curry
Asparagus/Green Beans
Strawberry Pie

**Week 5:** Pork Chops, Hot Beef, Grilled Cheese, French Dip, Porcupine Meat Balls, Shrimp Curry

## Bakery
(white bread)
<u>hard rolls</u>/or Kaiser
(soda crackers)

## Packaged Goods
(vinegar, lemon juice)
(Kitchen Bouquet sauce)
Worcestershire sauce
mayonnaise, salad croutons
favorite salad dressing
15 oz. tomato sauce
*26 oz. asparagus OR green
 beans
8 oz. lima beans
8 oz. cut green beans
16 oz. French-cut green beans
8 oz. red kidney beans
8 oz. kernel corn
8 oz. creamed corn
16 oz. applesauce
11 oz. mandarin oranges
26 oz. peach slices
26 oz. pears
26 oz. tomato soup
10 oz. cream of chicken soup
10 oz. cream of shrimp soup
*20 oz. beef broth OR
 2 env. beef au jus
box dry onion soup
3 oz. chicken-flavored
 Ramen noodles
(box quick white rice)
(box instant wild rice)
(box instant potatoes)

## Baking Goods
(sugar) (cornstarch, garlic)
(oil, Mrs. Dash)
celery salt & seeds
curry powder, paprika
Accent seasoning
vanilla, powdered sugar
3 oz. orange gelatin
3 oz. strawberry gelatin
graham cracker crust
4 oz. slivered almonds
4 oz. sunflower seeds

## Dairy
milk, eggs, butter
8 oz. cream cheese
9 oz. sour cream
12 oz. Cheddar cheese
16 oz. Velveeta cheese

## Frozen Foods
10 oz. cauliflower
16 oz. shrimp, deveined
8 oz. whipped topping

## Meat
16 oz. bacon
3 1/2 lb. beef roast
1 1/2 lb. ground beef
4-6 (1/2") pork chops

## Produce
3 tomatoes, 3 onions
celery, carrots, green pepper
cabbage, *spinach OR lettuce
3 apples, strawberries

# Day 1

## Grilled Pork Chops
**(Broiled)**

**4 to 6 (1/2" thick) pork
    chops**

**Salt & pepper**

1.    Grill or broil both sides until done (no pink shows when slit with knife.)

## Steamed Cauliflower

**1 pkg. frozen cauliflower
Salt & pepper**

**1/2 c. water**

1.    Use covered casserole dish.
2.    Microwave 7 minutes.

## Scalloped Corn

**8 oz. whole kernel corn
2 T. celery
2 T. onion**

**1/2 tsp. salt
1/8 tsp. paprika**

**SAUCE:
8 oz. creamed corn
1 egg, beaten**

**1/2 c. milk
2 tsp. sugar
Dash of Accent seasoning**

**1/2 c. bread or cracker
    crumbs**

**2 T. butter, melted
2 slices Velveeta cheese**

1.    Use casserole dish.
2.    Microwave frozen corn ingredients 7 minutes, otherwise combine corn ingredients.
3.    In medium bowl, combine sauce ingredients.
4.    Stir sauce and cheese slices into corn.
5.    Top with bread crumbs and melted butter.
6.    Bake at 350° for 1 hour.
7.    Freezes well if made ahead.

## Chilled Peaches

## Prepare for Day 2:

1.  Thaw beef roast.
2.  Use slow cooker tomorrow morning.
3.  Marinate Three-Bean Salad.
4.  Chill pears.

# Day 2

## Hot Beef Sandwiches
**(See Day 1 directions)**

3 1/2 lb. beef roast
1 T. Kitchen Bouquet
   browning sauce
Salt & pepper

2 T. oil
2 tsp. Mrs. Dash
1 env. dry onion soup
4 c. water

**White bread**

1. Brown thawed beef roast with oil in 5-quart pan.
2. Season with browning sauce and salt and pepper.
3. Cook in slow cooker, adding remaining ingredients.
4. Cook on HIGH 5 to 6 hours or on LOW 11 to 12 hours.
5. Slice cooked roast for sandwiches.
6. Save extra beef for Day 4.

## Instant Potatoes

1 box instant potatoes
Milk

Butter/margarine

1. Follow box directions for 4 to 6 servings of potatoes.

## Gravy

4 c. beef stock liquid
3 T. cornstarch

3/4 c. water

2. Microwave beef stock in glass casserole dish for 4 minutes.
3. Mix cornstarch and water separately.
4. Add 1/2 cornstarch mix to beef stock and stir.
5. Microwave on MEDIUM POWER for 2 minutes; stir.
6. Add remaining cornstarch mix and microwave 2 minutes.
7. Stir and cook on FULL POWER for 4 minutes.
8. If extra beef stock, hold for Day 4.

**Meat:**
9. Put beef sandwich and mashed potatoes on plate.
10. Pour gravy over both.

# Three-Bean Salad

1 (8 oz.) can lima beans
1 (8 oz.) can cut green
    beans

1 (8 oz.) can red kidney
    beans
1 onion, sliced into rings

SEASONINGS:
1/2 c. green pepper, diced
1/4 c. sugar

1 tsp. celery seed
2/3 c. vinegar
1/2 c. salad oil

1. Drain beans.
2. Put seasonings in pint jar. Cover and shake.
3. Combine all ingredients in covered plastic bowl.
4. Refrigerate.

# Chilled Pears

# Day 3

## Tomato Soup

**26 oz. tomato soup**
**1 can milk**

**Salt & pepper to taste**
**Crackers**

1. Use large casserole dish for soup.
2. Follow can directions, <u>but</u> add small portion of milk to tomato soup and stir to prevent clumps.
3. Add remaining milk; cover.
4. Heat in microwave on LOW for 4 minutes; stir.
5. Heat on MEDIUM POWER for 5 minutes, then on HIGH for 2 minutes.
6. Heat thoroughly.

## Grilled Cheese Sandwich

**2 slices bread per person**
**Butter**

**6 to 12 slices Velveeta**
**cheese**
**1 T. oil**

1. Use electric skillet.
2. Add oil.
3. Butter 2 slices of bread for each person.
4. Place 1 to 2 slices cheese between the two unbuttered sides of the bread.
5. Grill 2 minutes each side, so browned and the cheese has melted slightly.

## Apple Wedges

**Prepare for Day 4:**
1. Make Mandarin Orange Salad.

# Day 4

## French Dip Au Jus

**Beef slices**
**Hard rolls/Kaiser buns**
**Butter/margarine**

**2 env. beef au jus or large**
**can beef broth**

1. Warm beef slices in broth in 5-quart pan.
2. Add beef juice from Day 2.
3. Butter buns.
4. Make hot beef sandwiches.
5. Microwave sandwiches 30 seconds each.
6. Place on plate.
7. Pour 1/2 cup beef juice in individual Pyrex pudding dishes, or in soup bowls.

## Spinach or Lettuce Salad

**Spinach/Lettuce**
**1/2 onion, chopped**
**1 carrot, sliced**
**Croutons**

**3 tomatoes, cut in wedges**
**4 oz. Cheddar cheese, cubed**
**Favorite dressing**

## Mandarin Orange Salad

**3 oz. orange gelatin**
**1 c. boiling water**
**1 c. liquid (drained oranges**
**    + water)**

**1 carrot, shredded**
**11 oz. mandarin oranges**

**TOPPING:**
**1/4 c. mayonnaise**
**1/4 c. cream cheese**

**2 T. sugar**
**1 T. milk**

1. Boil water and add to gelatin in 7x9-inch glass serving dish.
2. Add liquid, carrots and mandarin oranges.
3. Cool and let set.

**Topping:**
4. Blend first 3 ingredients, stir in milk. Chill.

## Prepare for Day 5:

1. Thaw ground beef.
2. Prepare Ramen Noodle Salad.

# Day 5

## Porcupine Meatballs
**(See Day 4 for directions)**

**MEAT:**
1 1/2 lb. ground beef
1/3 c. chopped onion
1 tsp. salt

1/2 tsp. celery salt
1/8 tsp. garlic powder
1/8 tsp. pepper

**RICE:**
1/2 c. instant rice

1/2 c. water

**SAUCE:**
15 oz. tomato sauce
1 c. water

2 tsp. Worcestershire
   sauce

1.    Prepare rice according to box directions; cool.

**Meat:**
2.    Combine all ingredients.
3.    Add cooled rice.
4.    Shape into balls and place in covered casserole dish.
5.    Microwave for 3 minutes on FULL POWER; drain.
6.    Microwave for 2 minutes on FULL POWER; drain.

**Sauce:**
7.    Combine ingredients and pour over meat.
8.    Microwave on LOW POWER for 4 minutes, or until done <u>or</u> bake at 350°
      for 45 minutes, covered with foil, and then 15 minutes, uncovered.

# Ramen Noodle Salad

**1/4 head cabbage,
  shredded**

**1 pkg. sunflower seeds
1 pkg. slivered almonds**

**NOODLES:**
**1 (3 oz.) pkg. chicken Ramen
  noodles**

**DRESSING:**
**1 pkt. of Ramen seasoning**
**2 tsp. vegetable oil**

**4 tsp. sugar**
**3 tsp. white vinegar**

1.  Break noodles in half.
2.  Boil noodles in hot water; drain.
3.  Rinse in cold water; drain.
4.  Add remaining cabbage ingredients.
5.  Add mixed dressing; chill.

# Warmed Applesauce

1.  Sprinkle with cinnamon.
2.  Cover and microwave for 2 minutes.

## Prepare for Day 6:
1.  Prepare Strawberry Pie.
2.  Boil eggs 20 minutes, then place in cold water.
3.  Shell them immediately; cover and refrigerate.

# Day 6

## Shrimp Curry

Sauté:
1/4 c. butter

1/2 c. onion, chopped

1 box wild rice

1 (10 oz.) can cream of
    shrimp/chicken soup
1/3 tsp. curry powder

16 oz. frozen shrimp
1 tsp. salt
1/4 tsp. pepper

2 T. sour cream (opt.)

**GARNISH:**
3 boiled eggs, chopped

8 slices bacon, sprinkles

1. Defrost shrimp.
2. Fry bacon; drain. Cool and crumble.
3. Boil egg 10 minutes. Cool in water. Peel. Chop.
4. Sauté butter and onion.
5. Mix soup with curry powder and add to sauté.
6. Add thawed shrimp and cook.
7. When heated thoroughly, mix in sour cream.
8. Heat.
9. Serve over wild rice.
10. Garnish with chopped egg and bacon.
    (Add more curry powder for hot, spicy flavor.)


## Asparagus or Green Beans

2 (17 oz.) cans asparagus/or French-cut green beans

# Strawberry Pie

**(See Day 5 for directions)**

**Prepared graham cracker     OR**
    **pie crust**

**8 lg. graham crackers, crushed**
**1/4 c. sugar**
**6 T. margarine**

**FRUIT FILLING:**
**1/4 c. sugar**
**1 1/4 c. boiling water**

**3 oz. strawberry Jello**
**Fresh strawberries**

**CREAM FILLING:**
**3 oz. cream cheese,**
    **softened**
**1 tsp. vanilla**
**1 tsp. lemon juice**

**Dash of salt**
**1/3 c. powdered sugar**
**1 1/4 c. nondairy whipped**
    **topping**

1. Pie crust should be baked and cooled.
   (If making your own crust, bake in pie plate at 375° for 7 minutes.)
2. Prepare fruit filling by combining the first 3 ingredients and briefly chill in freezer.
3. Prepare cream filling by combining the first 5 ingredients. Gradually add whipped topping.
4. Put thin layer of cream filling over crust.
5. Top with sliced strawberries and 1/2 of gelatin mixture.
6. Chill in freezer about 10 minutes, until "set".
7. Spread rest of cream filling.
8. Layer with sliced strawberries and gelatin.
9. Chill.
10 Serve with whipped topping around the edges or on top.

## Prepare for Week 6:

1. Thaw turkey in cold water.
2. Refrigerate when thawed.

# Notes & Recipes

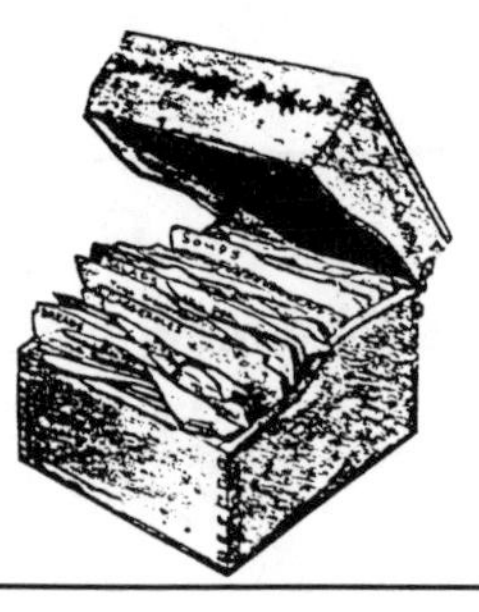

# Week Six

**Day 1** Turkey
Turkey Dressing
Sweet Potatoes
French Green Bean Casserole
Assorted Melons

**Day 2** Tacos
Refried Beans
Taco Chips with Dip

**Day 3** Barbecue Ribs
Baked Potatoes
Peas and Onions
Pears

**Day 4** Turkey Dressing Casserole
Corn
Blueberry Fruit Dessert

**Day 5** Taco Salad

**Day 6** Ham and Bean Soup
Cornbread
Relishes
Mandarin Pudding Dessert

## Week 6:  Turkey, Tacos, BBQ Ribs, Turkey Casserole, Taco Salad, Ham and Bean Soup

### Bakery
(soda crackers)
bag dried bread pieces

### Baking Goods
(sugar, flour, baking powder)
(cinnamon, sage)
brown sugar, marjoram
thyme, poultry seasoning
3 oz. instant vanilla pudding
16 oz. mini marshmallows
4 oz. pecans

### Dairy
(milk, butter) eggs
8 oz. Cheddar cheese
4 oz. sour cream
16 oz. Velveeta
*soft taco shells

### Frozen Foods
10 oz. corn
10 oz. peas and carrots
8 oz. whipped topping

### Produce
4 to 6 potatoes, 3 onions
celery, carrots
2 green peppers, radishes
4 tomatoes, lettuce
cantaloupe, honeydew,
   watermelon

### Packaged Goods
barbecue sauce
20 oz. French-style green beans
23 oz. sweet potatoes
3 oz. dried onion rings
11 oz. mandarin oranges
26 oz. pears
16 oz. crushed pineapple
15 oz. blueberries
10 oz. cream of celery soup
10 oz. cream of chicken soup
10 oz. golden mushroom soup
26 oz. chicken broth
chicken bouillon cubes
2 bottles taco sauce
16 oz. picante sauce
env. taco seasoning
*OR taco hard shells
10 oz. refried beans
6 oz. navy beans or mixed
24 oz. cornmeal
lg. taco chips
Fritos or sm. taco chips

### Meat
3 lb. ground beef
1 lb. pork sausage
4-6 country-style ribs
*small picnic ham OR bone
8 to 10 lb. turkey

### Paper
paper towels

# Day 1

## Stuffed Turkey

**Giblets, chopped**
**1 lb. sausage**

**2 tsp. chicken bouillon**
**2 c. water**

**SAUTÉ:**
**1/4 c. butter/margarine**
**1/4 c. onion, diced**

**2 celery stalks, diced**

**SEASONINGS:**
**1 tsp. thyme**
**1 tsp. marjoram**

**1 tsp. poultry seasoning**
**1 tsp. sage**

**5 to 6 c. dried bread**

**TURKEY:**
**8 to 10 lb. turkey, thawed**

**Stuffing:**
1. Rinse turkey with water.
2. Take out bag of giblets.
3. Rinse inside the turkey and rinse giblets.
4. Cook giblets in small pan with 2 cups water (save water).
5. Cook sausage in skillet; drain.
6. Add seasonings and sauté.
7. Add croutons with cooked and chopped giblets, and water.

**Turkey:**
8. Stuff turkey with dressing.
9. Follow cooking time on bird.
10. Spread with cooking oil.
11. Place turkey, breast-side up, in uncovered roasting pan. Roast at 325° for about 4 to 4 1/2 hours.
12. Baste hourly from bird's own juices.

# Sweet Potatoes

1 (23 oz.) can sweet
   potatoes
1/2 c. brown sugar

1/4 c. butter/margarine
1 c. mini marshmallows

1.   Cover casserole dish.
2.   Bake at 325° for 45 minutes, <u>or</u> microwave 7 minutes without marsh-mallows.

# French Green Bean Casserole

2 (8 oz.) cans French-cut
   green beans
1 (10 oz.) can golden
   mushroom soup

1 (3 oz.) can dry onion
   rings

1.   Mix beans and soup.
2.   Top with onion pieces.
3.   Bake, uncovered, at 325° for 45 minutes.

# Cantaloupe, Honeydew and Watermelon

**Prepare for Day 2:**
1.   Thaw ground beef.

# Day 2

## Tacos (See Day 1)

3 lb. ground beef
1/2 onion, diced
2 tsp. salt

1 tsp. pepper
1 pkg. taco seasoning

**Favorite taco sauce**

**FILLING:**
1/2 onion, diced
2 tomatoes, diced
1 green pepper, diced

1/2 lb. Cheddar cheese,
   shredded
1 head lettuce
8 to 12 soft OR hard shells

**Meat:**
1. Brown ground beef in skillet with onion, salt and pepper.
2. Drain.
3. Add taco seasoning; follow directions.
4. Fill shells with various fillings and serve with taco sauce.
5. Save meat for Day 5.

## Refried Beans

1 (10 oz.) can refried beans

1/4 c. water

1. Mix, cover, and microwave for 2 minutes.

## Taco Chips

1 pkg. taco chips
1 (16 oz.) pkg. Velveeta cheese

1 (16 oz.) jar picante
   sauce, blended

1. Melt cheese in microwave on LOW for 2 minutes.
2. Add picante sauce; stir.
3. Cover and heat on MEDIUM for 4 minutes; stir.
4. Heat thoroughly.
5. Serve hot with chips.

## Assorted Melons

(See Day 1)

## Prepare for Day 3:

1. Thaw country-style ribs.
2. Use slow cooker in morning!

# Day 3

## Barbecue Ribs

**4 to 8 country-style ribs**　　　　**1/2 c. water**
**3/4 c. barbecue sauce**

1.　Use slow cooker.
2.　Add thawed ribs and water.
3.　Pour sauce over meat.
4.　Cook on LOW heat all day.
5.　Check in evening and may need to turn to MEDIUM heat for 1 hour.

## Baked Potato

**4 to 6 potatoes**　　　　**Butter**
**4 to 8 oz. pkg. sour cream**

1.　Place between paper towels in microwave.
2.　Cook 4 minutes.
3.　Turn over.
4.　Cook 4 minutes.

## Peas and Onions

**1 pkg. frozen peas & onions**　　　　**1/4 c. water**

1.　Cover.
2.　Microwave 5 minutes.
3.　Best if bright green in color.

## Pears

**1 (26 oz.) can pears**

## Prepare for Day 4:
1.　Make blueberry dessert.

# Day 4

## Turkey Dressing Casserole

**Turkey Pieces from Day 1**
**1 (10 oz.) can cream of**
   **chicken soup**

**1 (10 oz.) can cream of**
   **celery soup**
**Turkey Dressing mix from**
   **Day 1**

1. Mix soups in bowl.
2. Use a 9x13-inch pan and layer turkey, soup, and dressing.
3. Bake at 350° for 40 minutes.

## Corn

## Blueberry Fruit Dessert

**BATTER:**
**1 c. flour**
**1 tsp. baking powder**
**1/2 c. sugar**

**1/2 c. milk**
**1 egg, beaten**
**2 T. butter/margarine**

**FRUIT:**
**1 (15 oz.) can blueberries,**
   **drained (OR favorite fruit,**
   **drained)**

**TOPPING:**
**1/2 c. sugar**

**2 tsp. cinnamon**

1. Use a 9x13-inch pan.
2. Place fruit on bottom of pan.
3. Sprinkle with mixed sugar and cinnamon.
4. Pour batter on top.
5. Bake at 350° for 25 minutes.

## Prepare for Day 5:
1.   Thaw ground beef.

## Prepare for Day 6:
1.   Thaw ham bone.
2.   Soak beans in water overnight.

# Day 5

## Taco Salad
**(See Day 2 for meat)**

**FILLING:**
**Lettuce, shredded**
**1 onion, diced**

**2 tomatoes, diced**
**1 green pepper, diced**
**1 bottle taco sauce**

**CHIPS:**
**1 pkg. taco chips, broken**

1. Use chilled meat from Day 2.
2. Mix meat and filling.
3. Top each serving with broken chips.

## Prepare for Day 6:
1. Drain beans.
2. Prepare soup and simmer 2 1/2 to 3 hours.
3. Make Mandarin pudding dessert.

# Day 6

## Ham and Bean Soup

2 c. beans (1 to 7 kinds)

26 oz. chicken broth

Crackers

**MEAT:**
2 c. ham pieces

1 1/2 c. carrots, diced

1 c. celery, diced

1/4 c. onion, diced

1.   Simmer meat and beans for 2 1/3 to 3 hours.

## Cornbread

Cornmeal

Eggs

1.   Follow package directions for baking in a 9x9-inch pan.

## Relish Plate

4 carrots (3" strips)

3 celery stalks (3" strips)

1 pkg. radishes

## Mandarin Pudding Dessert

1 (3 oz.) pkg. instant
  vanilla pudding

16 oz. pineapple, crushed

11 oz. mandarin oranges

6 oz. mini marshmallows

8 oz. whipped topping

4 oz. pecans

1.   Use a 9x9-inch dish.
2.   Prepare pudding according to directions.
3.   Mix pudding with undrained cans of fruit.
4.   Add remaining ingredients and stir.
5.   Garnish with pecans and chill.

## Prepare for Week 7:

1.   Thaw chicken breasts.

# Notes & Recipes

# *What Shall We Have for Dinner?*

## What to Serve with Chicken

| | |
|---|---|
| ROAST CHICKEN | Candied sweet potatoes, cauliflower |
| FRIED CHICKEN | Lima beans, mashed potatoes, corn on the cob and biscuits |
| CHICKEN FRICASSEE | Dumplings, corn on the cob |
| CHICKEN PIE | Green peas, tossed salad |
| CHICKEN SALAD | Potato chips, celery, pickles and peas |

## What to Serve with Fish

| | |
|---|---|
| TROUT | Potatoes diced in cream, asparagus, pickle |
| BAKED SNAPPER | Broccoli with Hollandaise sauce, mashed potatoes, tossed salad |
| LOBSTER | Steamed clams, baked potato |
| LOBSTER NEWBURG | French fried onions, watermelon pickle |
| FRENCH FRIED SHRIMP | Mixed vegetable, tomato and onion salad |
| BROILED FILLETS | Baked potatoes, scalloped tomatoes |
| CODFISH CAKES | Baked beans, bacon, green salad |
| CREAMED SALT COD | Boiled potatoes, coleslaw, toast and green salad |
| FILET OF SOLE | Coleslaw or dill pickles, tartar sauce |
| BAKED SALMON | Hollandaise sauce, mashed potatoes, peas |
| BROILED HALIBUT | Broccoli, corn fried in butter |
| FRIED FISH | French fried potatoes, tossed salad |
| SCALLOPED OYSTERS | Hash brown potatoes, broccoli |

# Week Seven

**Day 1** Chicken Cordon Bleu
Franciscan Mixed Vegetables
Apple Crisp

**Day 2** Hot Ham and Cheese Sandwiches
Pea Salad

**Day 3** Beef Stroganoff
Cooked Carrots
Lemon Pudding Salad

**Day 4** Minute Steak
Mixed Vegetables
Lettuce, Cottage Cheese, Peach Slices

**Day 5** Microwaved/Broiled Fish
Cut Green Beans
Macaroni and Tomatoes/Macaroni and Cheese
Orange Slices

**Day 6** Cold Shaved Ham Sandwiches
Potato Soup
Grapes

**Week 7:** Cordon Bleu, Hot Ham and Cheese, Stroganoff, Minute Steak, Fish, Potato Soup

## Bakery
sesame seed buns
Hoagie buns

## Dairy
(eggs, butter)
20 oz. milk
16 oz. cottage cheese
6 oz. sharp Cheddar cheese
4 oz. sour cream
Swiss cheese slices
American cheese slices
16 oz. Velveeta cheese

## Frozen Foods
10 oz. mixed vegetables
10 oz. Franciscan vegetables
10 oz. peas
20 oz. pollock/codfish
8 oz. whipped topping

## Meat
2 1/2 lb. shaved ham
1 1/2 lb. round steak
4 to 6 minute steaks
4 to 6 chicken breats, deboned

## Baking Goods:
4 oz. small marshmallows
1 pkg. instant lemon pudding
dill weed

## Packaged Goods
(pickles, mayonnaise)
(teriyaki, soy sauce)
(lemon juice, vinegar)
hot pepper sauce
26 oz. tomatoes
16 oz. green beans
26 oz. peach slices
16 oz. pineapple chunks
16 oz. crushed pineapple
10 oz. cream of celery soup
cream of chicken soup
beefy mushroom soup
20 oz. potato soup
dry onion soup mix
stroganoff sauce mix
box instant wild rice
8 oz. wide noodles
8 oz. elbow macaroni

## Produce
4 tomatoes
onion, celery, lettuce
pkg. baby carrots
3 oranges, 5 apples
grapes

# Day 1

## Chicken Cordon Bleu

**SAUCE:**

**1 pkg. dry onion soup**
**1 can cream of chicken**
   **soup**

**1 can cream of celery soup**
**1 box instant wild rice**
**1 can water**

**6 chicken breasts,**
   **skinned & deboned**

**Salt & pepper**

1. Use a 9x13-inch pan.
2. Mix sauce ingredients with rice and water.
3. Pour in bottom of pan.
4. Place chicken breasts on top and season.
5. Bake at 350° for 1 hour, covered with foil.
6. Bake 30 minutes, uncovered.
7. Chicken breasts can be purchased already skinned and deboned in meat department.

## Franciscan Mixed Vegetables

**10 oz. frozen Franciscan**
   **vegetables**

1. Microwave in covered dish for 7 minutes.

## Apple Crisp

**5 apples, peeled & sliced**
**3/4 c. sugar**
**3/4 tsp. cinnamon**

**3/4 c. flour**
**6 T. butter**

1. Use a 9x9-inch baking dish.
2. Place apples in the bottom.
3. Mix sugar, cinnamon and flour.
4. Cut in butter until crumbly.
5. Sprinkle over the apples.
6. Bake at 350° for 45 minutes.

## Prepare for Day 2:

1.    Make pea salad.

# Day 2

## Hot Ham and Cheese Sandwiches

1 1/2 lb. shaved ham
4 to 6 Swiss cheese slices

Sesame seed buns
Butter/margarine

1. Microwave ham on covered plate for 3 minutes.
2. Butter buns.
3. Place on coated pan on medium heat until slightly browned.
4. Make sandwiches with meat and cheese.
5. Melt cheese on sandwich in microwave.

## Pea Salad (See Day 1 for directions)

10 oz. frozen peas
1 c. cubed Cheddar cheese
2 hard-cooked eggs,
   chopped

1/4 c. celery, diced
2 T. onion, diced

Lettuce leaves

4 to 6 med. tomatoes

DRESSING:
1/3 c. mayonnaise
1/2 tsp. salt
1/8 tsp. pepper

1/4 tsp. bottled hot pepper
   sauce
Mrs. Dash

1. Boil eggs for 20 minutes, covered with water. Drain; cool in cold water, shell, and refrigerate.
2. Microwave peas with 1/4 cup water in casserole dish for 4 minutes (bright green yet). Drain and cool.
3. Add chopped eggs, celery, onions and cheese to peas.
4. Mix dressing in separate bowl. Add to above.
5. Place lettuce leaves on plates.
6. Cut each tomato in eighths.
7. Place each tomato on lettuce leaf.
8. Fill with pea salad.

## Prepare for Day 3:
1. Thaw round steak.
2. Marinate in morning.
3. Prepare lemon pudding salad.

# Day 3

## Beef Stroganoff

**MEAT:**

1 1/2 lb. steak (round,
flank, sirloin <u>or</u> 1 1/2 lb.
ground beef)

1 to 2 pkg. stroganoff
sauce mix
1/4 c. teriyaki sauce mix

Milk

4 oz. sour cream

**SERVE WITH:**
**6 oz wide noodles**

1. Marinate steak overnight or 1 hour.
2. Cut steak in strips and brown in fry pan.

**Noodles:**
3. In 3-quart pan, boil water.
4. Add noodles and cook until tender.
5. Drain and add cool water to remove paste; drain.
6. Place in covered glass casserole dish.

**Sauce:**
7. Remove meat from pan.
8. Make sauce from package ingredients; add to meat.
9. Mix in sour cream.
10. Heat thoroughly.
11. Warm noodles in microwave.
12. Serve meat on individual plates with noodles.

## Cooked Carrots

1 pkg. baby carrots
3 T. butter

1/2 c. onion, diced

**SEASONINGS:**
**Salt & pepper**

**Dill weed**

1. Place carraots, butter and onions in shallow baking dish.
2. Sprinkle with seasonings.
3. Cover and microwave for 7 minutes on FULL power.
   OR sauté on stove.

# Lemon Pudding Salad

**1 pkg. lemon pudding**
**8 oz. whipped topping**

**8 oz. crushed pineapple**
**6 oz. mini marshmallows**

1.   Mix and refrigerate.

## Prepare for Day 4:
1.   Thaw minute steaks.
2.   Chill peaches.

# Day 4

## Minute Steak

**6 minute steaks, browned**
**Salt & pepper**

**1 (10 oz.) can beef &**
**mushroom soup**

1. Use electric skillet.
2. Brown minute steaks.
3. Remove from heat.
4. Pour soup in pan, stir and cook 2 minutes.
5. Add minute steaks and simmer.

## Mixed Vegetables

**10 to 16 oz. frozen, mixed**
**vegetables**

**1/4 c. water**

1. Microwave for 7 minutes in covered dish.

## Lettuce Leaf, Cottage Cheese, Peach Slices

**1 head of lettuce**
**1 (24 oz.) ctn. cottage**
**cheese**

**1 (26 oz.) can peach**
**slices, drained**

1. On a leaf of lettuce, use ice cream scoop for topping with cottage cheese.
2. Arrange peach slices on the side.

**Prepare for Day 5:**
1. Thaw fish.

# Day 5

## Microwaved/Broiled Fish

**24 oz. frozen pollock/cod fish**
**3 T. melted butter**

**1 T. lemon juice**
**Salt & pepper to taste**

1. Combine butter and juice.
2. Baste on thawed fish.
3. Cover with plastic wrap.
4. Microwave 4 minutes each side; baste.
5. Check for doneness.
6. Microwave 4 minutes.

## Green Cut Beans

**1 (16 oz.) can green beans**

1. Heat in pan.

## Macaroni and Tomatoes

**8 oz. elbow macaroni**
**26 oz. tomatoes, blended**

**1 tsp. salt**
**1/8 tsp. pepper**

1. Boil water.
2. Add macaroni and stir.
3. Cook macaroni and rinse in cool water.
4. Drain again.
5. Add blended tomatoes and seasonings.
6. Simmer 15 to 20 minutes.

**VARIATION (Macaroni and Cheese):**
7. Rinse cooked macaroni in cool water.
8. Add 1/4 cup butter, 1/2 cup milk and 6 slices Velveeta cheese.
9. Cook on low heat, or microwave in covered dish on low heat.

## Orange Slices

# Day 6

## Potato Soup

**2 (10 oz.) cans potato
  soup**

**20 oz. milk**

1.  Prepare according to directions <u>or</u> microwave on LOW 3 minutes.
2.  Stir.
3.  Microwave on HIGH 4 minutes.
4.  Stir.
5.  Microwave on HIGH 2 minutes.

## Shaved Ham Sandwiches

**1 1/2 lb. shaved ham
4 to 8 Hoagie buns
6 slices soft cheese**

**Butter, mayonnaise,
  mustard, lettuce**

1.  Serve cold sandwiches.

## Grapes

## Prepare for Week 8:

1.  Thaw ground beef and sausage.

# Notes & Recipes

# Week Eight

**Day 1** Spaghetti
Garlic Bread
Lettuce Salad

**Day 2** Vegetable Burger
Onion Rings
Orange Gelatin Dessert

**Day 3** Cajun Bean Soup
Waldorf Salad

**Day 4** Fried Catfish/Cod
Lemon Rice & Orange Slices
Brussels Sprouts

**Day 5** Ham Logs
Macaroni and Cheese
Peas
Banana Bread

**Day 6** Broiled Chicken
California Mixed Vegetables
Hashbrowns

**Week 8:** Spaghetti, Vegetable Burger, Cajun Soup, Fish, Ham Logs, Chicken

## Bakery
garlic bread
sesame seed buns

## Baking Goods
(sugar, oregano, oil)
(baking soda, garlic)
flour, brown sugar
parsley, paprika
lemon pepper
dry mustard
Italian seasoning
Cajun seasoning
lg. marshmallows
3 oz. orange gelatin
3 oz. lemon gelatin
4 oz. walnuts
*4 oz. pecans

## Dairy
milk, eggs
3 oz. cream cheese
4 oz. sharp cheese
Velveeta cheese

## Frozen Foods
10 oz. Brussels sprouts
10 oz. California vegetables
10 oz. peas
10 oz. okra
breaded onion rings
20 oz. cod fillets
8 oz. whipped topping
16 oz. hashbrowns

## Packaged Goods
(ketchup, mustard)
(lemon juice, vinegar)
(mayonnaise)
Italian dressing
16 oz. stewed tomatoes
12 oz. tomato paste
23 oz. tomato juice
29 oz. tomato sauce
8 oz. crushed pineapple
20 oz. tomato soup
32 oz. chicken broth
16 oz. chicken broth
chicken bouillon granules
dry onion soup mix
dry black-eyed peas
dry Northern beans
box quick white rice
spaghetti noodles
*box macaroni and cheese OR
    8 oz. elbow macaroni
box graham crackers

## Produce
2 tomatoes
2 onions, celery, carrots
Bermuda (red) onion
lettuce, 3 ripe bananas
2 apples, 3 oranges

## Meat
3 1/2 lb. ground beef
1 lb. ground Italian sausage
3 to 5 lb. cut-up chicken
*2 lb. ham loaf OR
    (1 1/2 lb. ground ham)
    (1 lb. ground pork)
    (1/2 lb. ground beef)
1 to 2 ham steaks

# Day 1

## Spaghetti
Clark Wadle

**SAUCE:**
**29 oz. tomato sauce**
**12 oz. tomato paste**
**12 oz. water**

**23 oz. tomato juice**
**2 tsp. oregano**
**2 tsp. garlic powder**
**2 tsp. REAL* Italian seasoning**

**MEAT:**
**2 lb. ground beef**
**1 lb. Italian sausage**

**2 tsp. salt**
**1 tsp. pepper**
**1 med. onion, diced**

**8 oz. pkg. spaghetti noodles**
   **(good quality)**

1. Prepare sauce and simmer.
2. Brown meats, onions and seasonings.
3. Drain.
4. Add to sauce and simmer.
5. Boil water, add noodles, turn off heat and let stand for 20 minutes.
6. Stir several times.
7. Drain.
8. Rinse in cold water; drain.
9. Before serving, add hot water and drain, <u>or</u> microwave in covered dish.

## Lettuce Salad

**1 head lettuce (torn)**
**Italian dressing**

1. Save 6 lettuce leaves for Day 2.

## Garlic Bread

**1 loaf garlic bread**
**1/2 c. soft butter**

**1 T. garlic powder**

1. Mix garlic powder with soft butter.
2. Spread on slices of bread.
3. Broil carefully for a few minutes.

*Graziano Bros., 1601 South Union Street, Des Moines, IA 50315. Phone:
   515-244-7103.

## Prepare for Day 2:
1.   Thaw ground beef.
2.   Make Orange Gelatin Dessert.

## Prepare for Day 3:
1.   Soak black-eyed peas and beans in water overnight.

# Day 2

## Vegetable Burger

1 1/2 lb. ground beef

1 pkg. dried onion soup

Hamburger buns with
    sesame seeds

**CONDIMENTS:**

6 slices tomato

6 onion rings

6 lettuce leaves

Ketchup & mustard

1. Mix ground beef and dried soup into patties.
2. Broil, grill or fry burgers.
3. Serve with condiments on bun.

## Onion Rings

1 pkg. frozen prepared onion rings

1. Fix according to package directions.

## Orange Gelatin Dessert

3 oz. orange gelatin

1 c. carrots, grated

2 c. water

1 c. crushed pineapple

13 lg. marshmallows

1/2 c. nuts (opt.)

3 oz. cream cheese,
    softened

1 c. non-dairy whipped
    topping

1. Boil water.
2. Add gelatin in medium dish and dissolve.
3. In a separate medium bowl, melt cream cheese and marshmallows on LOW power in the microwave.
4. Whip in marshmallows and cream cheese while hot.
5. Slowly add dissolved gelatin to cream cheese mixture, stirring constantly.
6. Chill until syrupy.
7. Add carrots, pineapple and nuts.
8. Fold in whipped topping.
9. Chill

## Prepare for Day 3:

1. Drain black-eyed peas.
2. Add chicken broth and boil for 1 hour.
3. Make Waldorf Salad.

# Day 3

## Cajun Bean Soup
**(See Day 1 and 2 for directions)**

1 c. black-eyed peas

1 c. Northern beans

32 oz. chicken broth

16 oz. tomatoes, blended

**VEGETABLES:**
2 c. carrots, diced
2 c. okra, diced
1 c. Bermuda onion, diced

1 T. oil
1 tsp. Cajun seasoning
2 c. ham steak, cubed

1. Soak peas and beans in water overnight.
2. Drain.
3. Add chicken broth and blended tomatoes, and cook 1 hour.
4. Fry vegetables and ham.
5. Add to soup and cook 30 minutes.

## Waldorf Salad

3 oz. lemon gelatin
3/4 c. boiling water
1/2 c. cold water

1/2 c. ice cubes
1 tsp. lemon juice
1/4 c. mayonnaise

**FRUIT MIX:**
1 apple, wedged

1 celery stalk, diced
1/4 c. walnuts (pieces)

1. Add boiling water to gelatin. Dissolve.
2. Serve in 9x9-inch dish.
3. Add water and ice cubes.
4. Remove unmelted ice.
5. Add lemon juice.
6. Mix in mayonnaise.
7. Add apples, cut in thin wedges, then cut in thirds again.
8. Add celery and walnuts.
9. Refrigerate.

## Prepare for Day 4:

1.	Thaw fish.

# Day 4

## Fried Codfish

**24 oz. cod fillets**
**2 eggs, beaten**
**3/4 c. flour**

**Salt & pepper**
**3 T. oil**

1. Dip each fillet into eggs.
2. Then roll in flour.
3. Fry in electric skillet with oil.
4. Salt and pepper each side before browning.

## Lemon Rice

**2 c. quick white rice**
**2 c. chicken broth**
**1 T. parsley flakes**

**1 T. margarine**
**1 tsp. garlic powder**
**1 tsp. lemon juice**

1. Boil broth.
2. Add all other ingredients.
3. Remove from heat and cover for 5 minutes.

## Brussels Sprouts

**1 pkg. Brussels sprouts**
**1/4 c. water**

**1 T. vinegar**

1. Simmer in covered pan for 20 minutes.
2. Salt and pepper to taste.

## Orange Slices

## Prepare for Day 5:
1. Thaw meat for ham logs.

# Day 5

## Ham Logs

**2 lb. ham loaf (prepared in meat market)**

**Barbecue sauce (See optional homemade recipe below)**

1. Shape in 3-inch loaves.
2. Makes 10.
3. Simmer in electric skillet with lid (or fry pan with splatter screen).
4. Drain, and top with barbecue sauce.
5. Simmer 10 minutes.

OPTIONAL: Make own Ham Logs

**1 1/2 lb. ground ham**
**1 lb. ground pork**
**1/2 lb. ground beef**

**1 c. graham cracker crumbs**
**1 eggs, beaten**
**1 c. milk**

**SAUCE:**
**10 oz. can tomato soup**
**1/2 c. brown sugar**

**2 tsp. dry mustard**
**4 tsp. vinegar**

1. Bake at 350° for 1 hour.
2. Put in rows of 3 across 9x9-inch pan.
3. Can make loaves ahead of time and freeze.

## Macaroni and Cheese
**(From scratch or box)**

**8 oz. elbow macaroni**
**1/4 c. 2% milk**

**5 slices soft cheese (Velveeta)**
**Salt & pepper**

1. Boil 1 quart of water (2-quart pan).
2. Add macaroni and cook about 15 minutes, stirring 2 times; drain.
3. Pour in casserole dish.
4. Add milk and cheese.
5. Salt and pepper.
6. Cook in microwave on LOW POWER 2 minutes, covered.
7. Stir, then cook on MEDIUM POWER for 5 minutes.

## Green Peas

# Banana Bread

2 c. sugar
1 c. oleo, softened

3 eggs, beaten
2 c. ripe bananas, mashed

**DRY INGREDPENTS:**
3 c. flour
1 tsp. soda

1 tsp. baking powder
1 tsp. salt
1 tsp. cinnamon

1/2 c. milk

1. In large bowl, blend sugar and oleo.
2. Blend in eggs, then bananas.
3. In separate bowl, mix dry ingredients.
4. Then add and stir to mixture.
5. Add milk and mix.
6. Grease and lightly flour 2 loaf pans and fill scant half-full.
7. Bake at 325° for about 1 hour.

# Prepare for Day 6:

1. Thaw cut-up chicken in a plastic bag.
2. Place in cold water.
3. Refrigerate when thawed.

# Day 6

## Broiled Chicken

**3 lb. cut-up chicken**
**Salt & pepper**

**Lemon pepper**
**Paprika**

1. Chicken may be skinned.
2. Salt and pepper.
3. Place on broiler pan and broil both sides of chicken until brown (about 10 minutes each).
4. Bake at 375° for 20 minutes.

## California Vegetable Mix

1. Microwave frozen vegetables in covered casserole dish for 7 minutes.

## Hash Browns

**16 oz. frozen hash browns**
**4 oz. sharp cheese,**
   **shredded**

**1 tsp. chicken bouillon**
   **granules**
**1/2 c. hot water**
**1 T. butter**

1. Use covered casserole dish.
2. Add hash browns and cheese.
3. Pour chicken bouillon with water over top.
4. Add butter.
5. Bake at 375° for 30 minutes.
6. Stir twice.

**Prepare for Week 9:**
1. Defrost pork.
2. Marinate with teriyaki sauce overnight in plastic container.
3. Prepare potatoes and carrots and refrigerate in covered container.

# Notes & Recipes

# A Guide to Table Setting
## Breakfast Setting

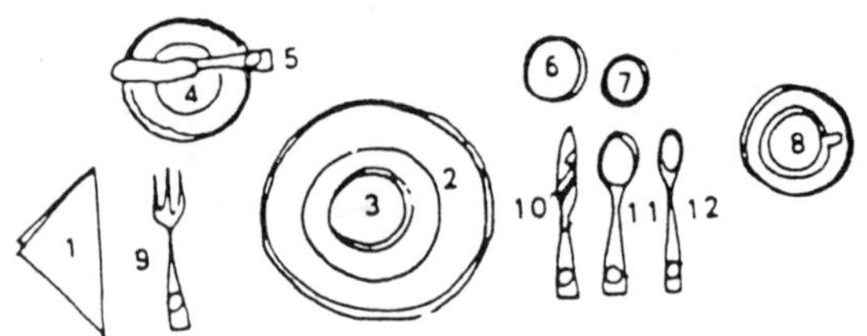

| | |
|---|---|
| 1. Napkin | 7. Juice glass |
| 2. Plate | 8. Cup and saucer |
| 3. Cereal dish | 9. Fork |
| 4. Bread-and-butter plate | 10. Knife |
| 5. Butter knife | 11. Cereal spoon (cream-soup spoon) |
| 6. Water glass | 12. Coffee or tea spoon |

## Luncheon/Informal Dinner Setting
### (First Course in Place)

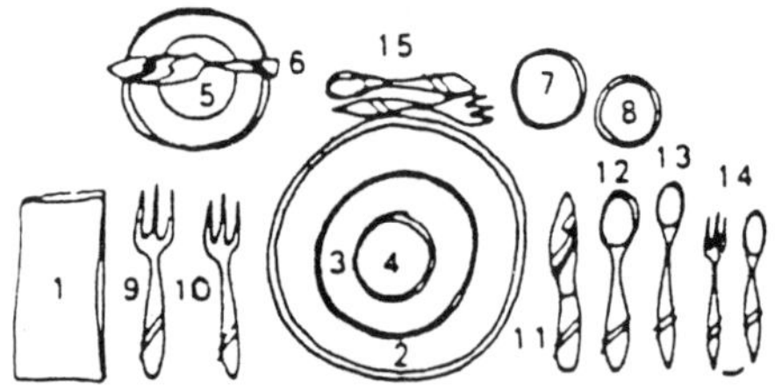

1. Napkin (should be placed across dinner plate if first course is omitted)
2. Plate
3. Liner plate for first course
4. Soup or seafood or fruit service
5. Bread-and-butter plate
6. Butter knife
7. Water glass or goblet
8. Wine goblet
9. Fork
10. Salad fork (may be placed to left of main course fork if salad is served before the main course)
11. Knife
12. Soup spoon (used if soup is served)
13. Coffee or tea spoon (may be brought in with coffee service)
14. Seafood fork or fruit cocktail spoon (used when a first course of seafood or fruit replaces soup)
15. Dessert silver (may be brought in with dessert service)

# Week Nine

**Day 1**  Boneless Pork Roast
Roasted Potatoes and Carrots
Asparagus/Brussels Sprouts
Warmed Applesauce

**Day 2**  Enchiladas
French-Cut Green Beans
Green Gelatin with Pears

**Day 3**  Fruit Plate
Italian Pasta Salad

**Day 4**  Beefburgers
Baked Beans
Macaroni and Cabbage Salad

**Day 5**  Pork Oriental Stir-Fry
Oriental Rice Pilaf
Fruit Cocktail Coffee Cake

**Day 6**  Tuna Salad Sandwiches
Can of Vegetable Soup
Apple

**Week 9:**  Pork Roast, Enchiladas, Beefburgers, Pork Stir-Fry, Tuna Sandwich, Pasta Salad

### Bakery
(soda crackers)
wheat bread
hamburger buns
fine, dry bread crumbs

### Packaged Goods
(teriyaki, soy sauce)
(mayonnaise, pickles)
15 oz. pitted ripe olives
French-cut green beans
*20 oz. asparagus
16 oz. pork and beans
23 oz. tomato juice
16 oz. tomato sauce
6 oz. tomato paste
16 oz. fruit cocktail
20 oz. pear chunks
20 oz. applesauce
11 oz. mandarin oranges
20 oz. pineapple chunks
20 oz. vegetable soup
10 oz. beef broth
14 oz. tuna
(box quick white rice)
8 oz. elbow macaroni
8 oz. thin spaghetti
jalapeños
*stir-fry sauce

### Meat
1 lb. bacon
3 lb. ground beef
4 lb. boneless pork roast

### Baking Goods
cumin
(sweet basil, garlic)
(brown sugar, oregano)
crushed red pepper
coconut, cornstarch
3 oz. lime gelatin
4 oz. walnuts

### Dairy
(milk, butter) eggs
10 oz. sharp Cheddar cheese
6 oz. heavy cream
3 oz. cream cheese
10" flour tortillas

### Frozen Foods
6 oz. pea pods
*10 oz. Brussels sprouts
6 oz. orange juice
8 oz. whipped topping

### Produce
5 lb. potatoes
4 onions, celery, carrots
3 green onions, lettuce
cabbage, cucumber
2 green peppers and 1 red
5 tomatoes, 4 apples
honeydew, cantaloupe and
grapes, 2 bananas

# Day 1

## Pork Roast

**(Cooking Time: 2 1/2 to 3 hours)**

**3 to 4 lb. boneless pork roast**
**1/4 c. water**

**2 T. Kitchen Bouquet browning sauce**
**1/4 c. teriyaki sauce**

1. Mix water with browning sauces.
2. Baste both sides of meat in roaster pan and add remaining sauce to pan.
3. Add remaining sauce to pan.
4. Bake at 450° for 20 minutes.
5. Turn meat over.
6. Reduce to 325° and bake 2 to 2 1/2 hours.
7. Baste with own juice every 30 minutes.
8. (Save 2 cups pork pieces for Day 4.)

## Roasted Vegetables

**8 potatoes, peeled & quartered**

**6 carrots, scraped**
**1 onion, quartered**

1. Add 1/2 cup water to roaster pan during last hour.
2. Add vegetables.
3. Salt and pepper to taste.

## Gravy

1. See directions on Week 1, Day 1.

## Asparagus or Brussels Sprouts

**20 oz. can asparagus**
**2 T. butter**

**1/4 c. onion, diced**

1. Use fry pan to cook onion and butter.
2. Pour over asparagus and microwave in covered dish for 7 minutes.
   OR

**10-ounce pkg. frozen Brussels sprouts**

1. Follow package directions..

# Warmed Applesauce

1. Microwave or heat with cinnamon sprinkled on top.

## Prepare for Day 2:
1. Thaw ground beef.

# Day 2

## Enchiladas

**SAUCE:**
16 oz. tomato sauce
1/2 tsp. crushed red pepper

1/2 tsp. cumin
1/4 tsp. salt
2 tsp. garlic powder

**MEAT:**
3 lb. ground beef

1 med. onion, diced
3/4 tsp. salt

6 to 10 (10") flour tortillas

10 oz. sharp cheese, shredded

1. Mix sauce ingredients in medium saucepan.
2. Simmer.
3. Brown ground beef with onion and salt. Drain.
4. Fill tortillas with meat.
5. Add 2 tablespoons sauce.
6. Roll up.
7. Place on serving plate.
8. Cover with plastic wrap.
9. Microwave 2 minutes.
10. Top with cheese.
11. Cook 1 minute.
12. Spoon sauce over individual enchiladas.
13. Save ground beef and sauce for Day 3.

## French-Cut Green Beans

1 (20 oz.) can French-cut green beans

1. Warm in pan on stove.

## Green Gelatin with Pears

3 oz. lime gelatin
20 oz. pear chunks

8 oz. whipped topping

1. Prepare gelatin according to box directions.
2. Pour into a 7x9-inch dish.
3. Add pear chunks and let set.
4. Spread layer of whipped cream on top.

## Prepare for Day 3:

1. Prepare pasta salad.
2. Chill pineapple chunks and mandarin oranges.

# Day 3

## Italian Pasta Salad

**VEGETABLES:**
5 tomatoes, chopped
2 green peppers, chopped

1 lg. onion, diced
15 oz. pitted ripe olives,
   sliced

1 pkg. spaghetti noodles
   (choose thin ones)

**SEASONING:**
2 to 4 T. jalapeños, diced
1 T. garlic powder
2 tsp. oregano
1 tsp. sweet basil

2 tsp. salt
1 tsp. pepper
3 T. salad oil
1 1/2 T. vinegar

1. Combine vegetables in large serving dish.
2. Combine seasonings in separate dish.
3. Add to vegetables.
4. Refrigerate.

**Noodles:**
5. Boil water in large saucepan.
6. Add noodles and stir several times.
7. Cook 20 to 25 minutes until tender.
8. Drain.
9. Add cold water.
10. Drain.
11. Cover.

12. Serve chilled vegetables over chilled noodles.

# Fruit Plate

**Lettuce leaves**
**20 oz. pineapple chunks**
**11 oz. mandarin oranges**

**Cantaloupe, honeydew,**
**  grapes**

***Later: 2 bananas, sliced**
**    (soak in lemon juice)**

**FRUIT DRESSING:**
**3 oz. cream cheese, softened**
**1/4 c. sugar**
**1/4 tsp. salt**

**1/4 c. heavy cream**
**1/4 c. pineapple juice**
**1/4 c. orange juice**
**2 T. lemon juice**

**Fruit Dressing:**
1. Use small serving bowl.
2. Blend sugar and salt with cream cheese.
3. Slowly add remaining ingredients while stirring constantly.
4. Refrigerate.

**Fruit:**
1. Place lettuce leaf on individual plates.
2. Combine pineapple chunks, mandarin oranges and grapes in large bowl.
3. Add favorite in-season fruit.
4. Top with sliced bananas before serving.
5. Top with fruit dressing.

# Prepare for Day 4:
1. Make macaroni salad.

# Day 4

## Beefburgers
**(See Day 2 for ground beef)**

**2 eggs, beaten**
**23 oz. tomato juice**
**1 c. enchilada sauce**
**1/2 c. dried bread crumbs**
    **(fine)**

**1 T. chicken bouillon**
    **granules**
**Hamburger buns**
**Pickles**
**Ketchup**
**Mustard**

1. Warm ground beef on LOW heat from Day 2.
2. Beat eggs with mixer in medium bowl.
3. Add juice and beat again.
4. Add to meat.
5. Add enchilada sauce to meat and simmer.
6. Add bouillon and bread crumbs.

## Baked Beans

**1 (16 oz.) can pork &**
    **beans**
**1 (3 oz.) can tomato paste**
**1/4 c. chopped onions**

**1/2 c. brown sugar**
**2 T. white sugar**
**4 slices bacon, cut up**

1. Mix in casserole dish and bake at 350° for 1 1/2 hours.

# Macaroni and Cabbage Salad

8 oz. elbow macaroni
2 c. cabbage, finely
    chopped
1/2 lg. cucumber, peeled &
    chopped

1/2 lg. green pepper,
    chopped
1/2 c. onion, diced

DRESSING:
1 c. mayonnaise
1/2 c. sugar

1/4 c. vinegar
1 tsp. salt
1/8 tsp. pepper

1. Boil water in large saucepan.
2. Add macaroni and stir.
3. Cook until tender; drain.
4. Add cold water.
5. Cool and drain.
6. Make dressing and chill.
7. Chop vegetables.
8. Add to macaroni in medium-size bowl.
9. Add dressing and stir.
10. Chill.

## Prepare for Day 5:

1. Make coffee cake.

# Day 5

## Pork Oriental Stir-Fry

**(Use pork from Day 1)**

2 c. roasted pork (chunks)
1/2 pkg. frozen pea pods
3 carrots, diagonally sliced

1/2 onion, sliced in rings
3 stalks celery, chopped
2 T. oil

**SEASONING SAUCE:**
2 T. water

2 T. soy sauce
1 T. cornstarch

1. Use electric skillet and fry pork from Day 1 until browned in oil.
2. Remove from pan.
3. Fry carrots, celery and onion on MEDIUM-HIGH for 3 minutes, turning once to brown.
4. Add pea pods and fry 2 minutes.
5. Add meat and warm through, with soy sauce added.
6. Before serving, combine sauce and pour over meat.
7. Cook and stir until coated, about 2 minutes.
* Can use purchased stir-fry sauce for individual servings.

## Oriental Rice Pilaf

1 c. beef broth
1 1/2 c. quick white rice
1/3 c. green onions,
    chopped
1/2 c. onions, diced

1/2 red pepper, chopped
1 tsp. garlic
1 tsp. parsley flakes
1 T. soy sauce
2 shakes red pepper flakes

1. Boil beef broth in medium saucepan.
2. Add all ingredients.
3. Remove from heat.
4. Cover and let stand 5 minutes.

# Fruit Cocktail Coffee Cake

**FROSTING:**
3/4 c. sugar
1/2 c. margarine

1/2 tsp. vanilla
1/4 c. milk

1/2 c. nuts, chopped

**CAKE:**
2 eggs
1 1/4 c. sugar
1 (16 oz.) can fruit cocktail,
    undrained

2 1/4 c. flour
1 1/2 tsp. soda
1/2 tsp. salt
1 tsp. vanilla

1/2 c. nuts, chopped

1. Make frosting first.
2. Boil ingredients 12 minutes on medium heat, stirring constantly.
3. Add nuts and cool.
4. Grease a 9x15-inch pan.
5. Cream eggs and sugar in medium bowl.
6. Add the next 5 ingredients and stir.
7. Pour into pan.
8. Sprinkle with nuts and coconut.
9. Bake at 350° for 30 minutes.
10. Cool.
11. Drizzle with frosting.

## Prepare for Day 6:
1. Boil eggs. Drain. Add cold water. Peel.
2. Refrigerate in plastic bag.

# Day 6

## Tuna Salad Sandwiches

2 (7 oz.) cans tuna
1/2 c. mayonnaise
3 celery stalks, diced
1/2 onion, diced

1/2 tsp. salt
1/4 tsp. pepper
2 slices toast per person
Lettuce leaves

**GARNISH:**
**Pickles**

1. Use medium bowl.
2. Mix the first 6 ingredients.
3. Toast bread and butter
4. Spread tuna mixture on each sandwich.
5. Add lettuce leaf.
6. Cut diagonally.

## Vegetable Soup

1 lg. can vegetable soup          Crackers

1. Add water and heat in large saucepan on stove.

## Apple

**Prepare for Week 10:**
1. Thaw 4 to 6 beef steaks.
2. Marinate steak overnight <u>or</u> for 1 hour.
3. Make orange pudding dessert.

# Notes & Recipes

# Week Ten

**Day 1** Beef Teriyaki Steak
Baked Potato
Fried Peppers, Onions and Mushrooms
Orange Pudding Dessert

**Day 2** Hamburger with Mushrooms
French Fries

**Day 3** Beef Fajitas
Cauliflower with Cheese
Rainbow Salad

**Day 4** Fried Walleye
Carrot and Rice Bake
Broccoli

**Day 5** Goulash
Green Beans with Onions
Pineapple Chunks

**Day 6** Mexican Ham Soup
Layer Lettuce Salad
Grapes

## **Week 10:** Steak, Hamburgers, Fajitas, Fish, Goulash, Mexican Soup

### **Bakery**
hamburger buns

### **Packaged Goods**
(teriyaki, soy sauce)
(lemon juice, mayonnaise)
20 oz. tomatoes
16 oz. tomatoes
20 oz. cut green beans
*8 oz. mushrooms
20 oz. pineapple chunks
10 oz. crushed pineapple
11 oz. mandarin oranges
10 oz. tomato soup
32 oz. chicken broth
16 oz. mixed dry beans
    (1-13 kinds)
(box quick white rice)
8 oz. elbow macaroni
12 oz. picante sauce
green chilies (opt.)

### **Frozen Foods**
10 oz. broccoli
10 oz. cauliflower
10 oz. peas
16 oz. French fries
20 oz. walleye/pollock
8 oz. whipped topping

### **Baking Goods**
(salt)
(pepper, flour, sugar)
(chili and garlic powder)
(paprika, oil)
3 oz. lime, lemon and
    strawberry gelatins
3 oz. instant lemon pudding
12 oz. mini marshmallows

### **Dairy**
milk, eggs, butter
Velveeta cheese
Swiss cheese slices
22 oz. Cheddar cheese
6 oz. guacamole dip
8 oz. sour cream
*10-inch flour tortillas OR
    4 to 8 pita shells

### **Meat**
(1 lb. bacon)
2 lb. beef round steak
4 beef steaks
3 lb. ground beef
*sm. picnic ham OR ham bone

### **Produce**
4 to 6 potatoes
4 onions, celery, carrots
2 green peppers and 1 red
lettuce, grapes
*fresh mushrooms

### **Other**
paper towels

# Day 1

## Beef Teriyaki Steak

**4 to 6 beef steaks**
**1/4 c. teriyaki sauce**

**2 T. soy sauce**
**Salt & pepper to taste**

1. Marinate steak.
2. Cover in plastic container.
3. Refrigerate.
4. Grill or broil steak, browning both sides.

## Baked Potatoes

**4 to 6 lg. potatoes**
**Sour cream**

**Salt & pepper**
**Paper towels**

1. Wash potatoes.
2. Poke with fork in 3 to 4 places on each potato.
3. Place between 2 paper towels in microwave.
4. Cook 5 minutes on HIGH.
5. Turn potatoes upside down.
6. Cook 3 to 5 more minutes.
7. Insert fork to check doneness.

## Fried Peppers, Onions and Mushrooms

**1/4 c. butter**
**Green pepper, cut in strips**
**Red pepper, cut in strips**

**1 lg. onion, cut in rings &**
**separated**
**Mushrooms**

1. Melt butter in large skillet.
2. Use splatter screen.
3. Add cut-up peppers and quickly fry and stir both sides on medium-high heat.
4. Add onions and mushrooms.
5. Fry an additional 5 minutes.
6. Serve as side dish to teriyaki steak.

# Orange Pudding Dessert

3 oz. lemon instant pudding
1 1/2 c. milk
1 1/2 c. non-dairy whipped
   topping

10 oz. mandarin oranges,
   drained
10 oz. crushed pineapple,
   drained
8 oz. mini marshmallows

1. Mix milk and pudding in large bowl.
2. Refrigerate until just slightly thick.
4.  Mix in other ingredients..
5. Chill.

## Prepare for Day 2:
1. Thaw ground beef.

# Day 2

## Hamburger with Mushrooms and Onions

**1 1/2 lb. ground beef**
**Salt & pepper**

**Hamburger buns**
**Swiss cheese**

Sauté:
**8 oz. sliced mushrooms**
**1 med. onion, sliced &**
    **separated**

**3 T. butter**

1. Grill, broil or fry hamburgers.
2. Meanwhile, sauté mushrooms and onions.
3. Melt cheese on burgers.
4. Add mushrooms and onions before serving sandwiches.

## French Fries

**1 pkg. frozen fries**

1. Follow package directions.

## Prepare for Day 3:

1. Thaw beef roast and marinate in the morning.
2. In morning make Rainbow Gelatin Salad.

# Day 3

## Beef Fajitas (See Day 2 directions)

2 lb. beef round steak
1/4 c. teriyaki sauce

2 T. soy sauce
2 tsp. garlic powder

Pita shells <u>or</u> 10 flour
    tortillas

TOPPINGS:
Lettuce, shredded
Sharp cheese, shredded
1 med. onion, diced

12 oz. picante sauce
8 oz. sour cream
6 oz. guacamole dip

1. Marinate steak in morning.
2. Grill or broil steak.
3. Slice in thin strips.
4. Each person fills own shells with desired toppings.

# Cauliflower with Cheese

16 oz. cut-up cauliflower

4 Velveeta cheese slices

1. Microwave cauliflower in casserole dish until almost tender (about 7 minutes).
2. Top with cheese slices.
3. Cover and cook just until melted.

# Rainbow Gelatin Salad

**GREEN LAYER:**
3 oz. lime gelatin

1 c. boiling water
1 c. ice cubes

**YELLOW LAYER:**
3 oz. lemon gelatin
1 c. boiling water

1 c. mini marshmallows
8 oz. crushed pineapple

**WHITE LAYER:**
1/2 c. non-dairy whipped
    topping

1/2 c. mayonnaise

**RED LAYER:**
3 oz. strawberry gelatin

1 c. boiling water
1 c. ice cubes

**4 to 6 lettuce leaves**

1. Use a 9x9-inch glass dish.
2. Pour in green layer.
3. Refrigerate until set.
4. Mix yellow layer.
5. Cool (don't let set).
6. Mix cooled yellow mixture with white layer.
7. Pour this over green layer.
8. Refrigerate until set.
9. Mix red layer.
10. Pour over yellow layer.
11. Chill.
12. Cut in squares and serve over lettuce leaves.

## Prepare for Day 4:
1. Thaw fish.

# Day 4

## Fried Walleye

**20 oz. walleye/pollock**

**2 eggs, beaten**

**BREADING MIX:**
**1 c. flour**
**2 tsp. paprika**

**1 tsp. salt**
**1/8 tsp. pepper**

1. Dip fish in eggs.
2. Then roll in breading mix.
3. Fry in electric skillet with 4 tablespoons oil, at 350°.
4. Brown each side.
   (Burn scented candle by fish to reduce odors.)

## Carrot and Rice Bake

**VEGETABLES:**
**3 c. carrots, shredded**
**1/2 c. onions, diced**
**1 T. butter**

**1 c. chicken broth**
**1 tsp. salt**
**1/8 tsp. pepper**

**1 c. quick white rice**

**1/2 c. milk**
**2 eggs, beaten**

**2 c. Cheddar cheese,**
**   shredded**

1. Simmer vegetables with seasonings in covered, medium saucepan for 15 minutes.
2. Use 9x9-inch casserole dish.
3. Put rice in bottom.
4. Beat eggs and milk together; add 1 1/2 cups cheese.
5. Pour over rice.
6. Pour vegetable mix over milk.
7. Top with 1/2 cup cheese.
8. Cover. Bake at 350° for 30 minutes.
9. Save remaining broth for Day 6.

# Broccoli

1. Steam cook or microwave until almost tender (it should still be bright green in color).

## Prepare for Day 5:
1. Thaw ground beef.

## Prepare for Day 6:
1. Thaw ham.
2. Rinse beans and drain.
3. Soak 2 cups beans in water.

# Day 5

## Goulash

**MEAT:**
**1 1/2 lb. ground beef**
**1/2 c. onion**

**2 tsp. salt**
**1/2 tsp. pepper**

**SAUCE:**
**1 (5 oz.) can tomato soup**

**1 (20 oz.) can tomatoes,**
   **puréed**

**1 c. elbow macaroni**

1.   Brown meat mixture; drain.
2.   Cook macaroni in boiling water until tender, 15 to 20 minutes; drain.
3.   Use blender on tomatoes.
4.   Combine meat, tomato sauce and macaroni.
5.   Cook on low heat for 35 minutes, in covered 5-quart pan.

## Green Beans with Onions

**20 oz. cut green beans**
**1/2 sm. sliced onion**

**1 tsp. salt**
**1/8 tsp. pepper**

1.   Cook all ingredients in medium-size covered saucepan.

## Pineapple Chunks

**Prepare for Day 6:**
1.   Make bean soup (3 hours).
2.   Add remaining broth from Day 4.
3.   Make layer salad.

# Day 6

## Mexican Ham Soup
**(See Day 5 directions)**

1 sm. picnic ham <u>OR</u> ham
   bone

2 c. beans (1 to 13 kinds)

8 to 10 c. water

1/2 lg. onion, chopped
1 (16 oz.) can tomatoes,
   blended
1 T. lemon juice
1/2 tsp. pepper

1 tsp. chili powder
1 sm. can green chilies,
   chopped (opt.)

1. Soak beans in water overnight; drain.
2. Boil beans in chicken broth for 1 1/2 hours.
3. Add remaining ingredients and simmer 30 minutes.
   (If hambone with less meat is used, replace some water with 32 ounces chicken broth.)

## Layer Lettuce Salad

1/2 head lettuce (torn)
1/4 c. diced green pepper
1/4 c. celery, diced

1/2 c. onion, diced
5 oz. frozen peas,
   uncooked

Mix:
1 T. sugar

1 c. <u>real</u> mayonnaise

4 to 5 oz. Cheddar cheese,
   shredded

4 slices bacon, fried crisp
   & crumbled

1. Use a 9x9-inch dish (Tupperware works best).
2. Layer each ingredient.
3. Cover and chill.

## Grapes

## Prepare for Week 11:
1. Thaw turkey.
2. Make cheesecake.

# Notes & Recipes

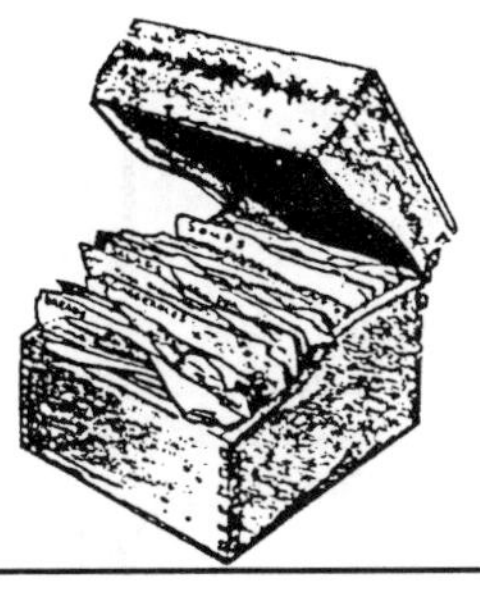

# Dietetic

## Foods To Be Avoided When Salt is Restricted

Sauerkraut or other vegetables
    prepared in brine
Breads and rolls with salt toppings
Potato chips
Pretzels
Salted popcorn
Salty or smoked meats
    Bacon
    Bologna
    Chipped or corned beef
    Frankfurters
    Ham
    Koshered meat
    Luncheon meats
    Salt pork
    Sausage
Salty or smoked fish
    Anchovies
    Caviar
    Salted or dried cod
    Herring
    Sardines
Processed cheese

Cheese spreads
Peanut butter
Salted nuts
Bouillon cube, regular
Catsup
Celery, garlic, or onion salt,
    except when used in cooking
    in place of regular salt
Chili sauce
Horseradish, prepared
Meat extracts
Meat sauces
Meat tenderizers
Monosodium glutamate
Mustard, prepared
Olives
Pickles
Relishes
Salt at the table
Salt substitutes, unless
    recommended by physician
Soy sauce
Worcestershire sauce

## Foods Which are Very Low in Sodium

Asparagus
Broccoli
Brussels sprouts
Cabbage
Cauliflower
Cucumbers

Escarole
Eggplant
Endive
Green beans
Green peppers
Lettuce

Mushrooms
Okra
Radishes
Summer squash
Tomatoes
Turnip greens

## Spices Give Taste To Low-Sodium Diet

Many Americans these days are being urged to cut back on their sodium intake — one of the most important of these reasons being the high cost of high blood pressure.

Luckily, however, giving up excess sodium doesn't have to mean giving up good taste. The test kitchen of the American Spice Trade Association has found that spices can do a lot to put enjoyment back in your mealtimes.

Spices themselves contain so little sodium that they can be used wherever salt has been reduced or cut out. One good idea is to keep a shaker of mixed spices at the table.

Here is one blend the spice kitchen suggests: 2 1/2 tsp. each of paprika, garlic powder, and powdered mustard; 5 tsp. of onion powder; 1/2 tsp. ground white pepper; and 1/4 tsp. celery seed.

# Week Eleven

**Day 1** Roasted Turkey
Lima Bean Casserole
Cherry Cheesecake

**Day 2** Stuffed Peppers/Stuffed Cabbage
Hot Dogs
5-Cup Fruit Salad

**Day 3** Seafood Linguini
Peas and Carrots
Tossed Salad

**Day 4** Turkey Sandwiches
Fried Cabbage, Peppers and Onions
Peaches

**Day 5** Taco Dinner
Burritos
Assorted Melons

**Day 6** Sliced Roast Beef Sandwiches
French Onion Soup
Macaroni and Cabbage Salad

**Week 11:** Turkey, Stuffed Peppers/Cabbage, Seafood Linguini, Turkey Sandwich, Mexican Dinner, French Onion Soup

## Bakery
wheat bread
hot dog buns
Hoagie buns

## Baking Goods
(sugar)
(Mrs. Dash) chili powder
celery salt, coconut
8 oz. mini marshmallows
box cheesecake mix
cherry pie filling

## Dairy
(milk, butter)
Swiss cheese slices
8 oz. shredded Cheddar cheese
4 oz. sour cream
10" flour tortillas
guacamole dip

## Frozen Foods
10 oz. lima beans
10 oz. broccoli
10 oz. cauliflower
10 oz. peas and carrots
8 oz. scallops
8 oz. imitation crab
4 oz. salad shrimp
8 oz. whipped topping

## Meat
hot dogs
3 lb. ground beef
1/2 lb. ground sausage
1 1/2 lb. pre-cooked,
   beef roast, sliced
8 to 10 lb. turkey

## Packaged Goods
(ketchup)
(mustard, lemon juice)
(pickles) salad croutons
(vinegar) mayonnaise
dill pickle relish
(jalapeños)
favorite salad dressing
16 oz. stew tomatoes
16 oz. taco sauce
3 oz. dry French onion rings
refried beans
4 oz. green chilies
26 oz. peaches
10 oz. pineapple tidbits
11 oz. mandarin oranges
cream of chicken soup
cream of mushroom soup
10 oz. cheese soup
*1 to 2 pkg. dry onion soup mix
   (OR 1 to 2 beef broth)
(chicken bouillon cubes)
*mushrooms (or fresh)
6 oz. crabmeat
(instant white rice)
16 oz. linguini noodles
8 oz. macaroni wheels
10 oz. corn chips
instant potatoes

## Produce
3 onions
green onions, lettuce
cherry tomatoes
*fresh mushrooms
1 green pepper
*5 to 7 green peppers OR
   head of cabbage
cantaloupe, honeydew,
   watermelon

# Day 1

## Roasted Turkey
**(See Week 6, Day 1 for directions)**

8 to 10 lb. turkey (save remaining turkey for Day 4)

## Lima Bean Casserole

| | |
|---|---|
| 10 oz. frozen lima beans | 1 (10 oz.) can cheese soup |
| 10 oz. frozen broccoli | 2 T. milk |
| 10 oz. frozen cauliflower | 1 (3 oz.) can French onion |
| 1 (10 oz.) can cream of | rings |
| mushroom soup | |

1. Microwave vegetables in casserole dish for 10 minutes; drain.
2. Mix soups with milk and pour over vegetables.
3. Bake at 350° for 30 minutes.
4. Cover with French onions and bake 10 minutes.

## Mashed Potatoes and Gravy
**(See Week 1, Day 1 for directions)**

## Cherry Cheesecake

| | |
|---|---|
| 1 box quick cheesecake | 1 (20 oz.) can cherry pie |
| | filling |

**Prepare for Day 2:**
1. Thaw ground beef
2. Prepare 5-Cup Salad.

# Day 2

## Stuffed Peppers/ Stuffed Cabbage

**4 to 6 lg. green peppers or
    head of cabbage**

**FILLING:**
**1 to 1 1/2 lb. ground beef**
**1/2 onion, diced**

**1 c. instant white rice**
**1 c. boiling water**
**1 (16 oz.) can stewed
    tomatoes (or 4 med.
    fresh)**

**2 tsp. salt**
**1 tsp. chili powder**
**1/8 tsp. pepper**

**4 oz. shredded sharp
    cheese**

1. Cook peppers in boiling salt water for 7 minutes.
2. Remove peppers, salt them and place in pan.
3. Meanwhile, brown meat filling in 5-quart pan.
4. Meanwhile, boil water, add rice and remove from heat; cover with lid
   for 5 minutes.
5. Combine meat, rice and tomatoes.
6. Fill each pepper, or fill cabbage leaf and roll up.
7. Top each pepper with cheese.
8. Extra filling can go in the bottom of pan.
9. Bake at 350° for 30 minutes.

## Hot Dogs (for kids)

**4 to 6 hot dogs**
**1 pkg. hot dog buns**

**Garnish: dill relish,
    mustard, ketchup**

1. Microwave for 1 to 2 minutes, <u>or</u> broil carefully.

# 5-Cup Fruit Salad

| | |
|---|---|
| **8 oz. non-dairy whipped topping** | **1 c. marshmallows** |
| **1 c. coconut** | **1 c. mandarin oranges, drained** |
| | **1 c. pineapple tidbits, drained** |

1. Mix together in medium bowl. Cover.
2. Refrigerate.

## Prepare for Day 3:
1. Thaw fish.

# Day 3

## Seafood Linguini

**8 oz. frozen scallops,
thawed
8 oz. frozen imitation
crabmeat**

**4 oz. frozen salad shrimp
1 (6 oz.) can crabmeat**

**SOUP MIX:
1 (10 oz.) can cream of
chicken soup/or shrimp
1/2 c. chicken broth**

**1/2 tsp. salt
1/4 tsp. pepper
3/4 tsp. lemon juice
1 tsp. garlic powder**

Sauté:
**1/2 onion, diced
1/4 c. butter**

**6 fresh mushrooms, sliced**

**10 to 12 oz. linguini noodles**

1. Use casserole dish.
2. Defrost fish.
3. Mix soup ingredients and stir into fish.
4. Microwave for 7 minutes.
5. Boil water in 5-quart pan and cook noodles about 15 minutes or until tender.
6. Drain noodles. Add cold water.
7. Sauté onions, butter and mushrooms.
8. Add to soup and fish.
9. Microwave 4 minutes.
10. Before serving, drain water off noodles.
11. Cover with hot water and drain, or leave 1/4 cup water in noodle dish; cover.
12. Microwave 2 minutes.

## Peas and Carrots

**10 oz. frozen peas & carrots**

1. Cook 5 minutes in covered saucepan, with 1/4 cup water.

# Tossed Salad

**Head of lettuce**          **Favorite salad dressing**
**Cherry tomatoes, halved**  **Croutons**
**4 green onions, diced**

1.   Tear lettuce and place in individual bowls.
2.   Place 4 to 5 tomato halves in each bowl.
3.   Sprinkle with green onions.
4.   Top with salad croutons and serve with favorite dressings.

## Prepare for Day 4:

1.   Chill peaches.

# Day 4

## Turkey Sandwiches
**(Use turkey from Day 1)**

Turkey slices
Hoagie sandwich buns

6 slices Swiss cheese

CONDIMENTS:
Pickles
Mustard

Mayonnaise
Lettuce
Tomatoes

1. Place turkey slices in bun.
2. Add cheese and microwave 30 seconds.
3. Top with favorite condiments.

## Fried Cabbage

1/2 head cabbage (chunks)
1/2 onion, sliced &
    separated

1 green pepper, chopped
1 T. oil

1. Put oil in pan.
2. Add other ingredients.
3. Fry and stir for 15 to 20 minutes.
   (It's great if slightly crunchy!)

## Peaches

**Prepare for Day 5:**
1. Thaw ground beef.

# Day 5

## Taco Dinner

**MEAT:**
1 lb. ground beef
1 med. onion, diced

1 (10 oz.) can chili beans

**VEGETABLES:**
1/4 head lettuce, shaved

2 to 3 tomatoes, chopped
1 med. onion, chopped

1 (10 oz.) pkg. corn chips
Taco sauce

6 oz. Cheddar cheese,
shredded

1. Brown meat and onions; drain.
2. Add chili beans and simmer.

**To serve:**
3. Put handful of corn chips (slightly crushed) on plate.
4. Put hamburger and beans on top.
5. Layer shaved lettuce.
6. Layer tomatoes.
7. Layer onions.
8. Spoon on taco sauce.
9. Top with shredded cheese.

# Burritos

**MEAT:**

1 lb. ground beef

1/2 lb. ground sausage

6 oz. refried beans

4 oz. taco sauce

Sauté:

1 green pepper, diced

4 oz. can green chilies, diced

1 med. onion, diced

1/4 c. butter

1 T. jalapeño, diced

5 lg. flour tortillas

**TOPPINGS:**

Sour cream, guacamole (opt.)

1. Brown meat; drain.
2. Add refried beans and taco sauce to meat and simmer.
3. Sauté onions, green chilies, green pepper, and jalapeño with butter.
4. Fill tortilla shells with meat mixture.
5. Add 1 tablespoon of fried vegetables and microwave 30 to 45 seconds.
6. Before serving, add 1 tablespoon sour cream and guacamole.

# Assorted Melons

Cantaloupe, honeydew, watermelon

# Day 6

## French Onion Soup

**2 pkg. French onion soup mix**

**4 to 6 slices Swiss cheese**
**1 c. salad/soup croutons**

1. Follow directions on package of soup.
2. Add croutons and cook.
3. Put soup into individual bowls.
4. Microwave slice of cheese in each bowl for 20 seconds.

## Sliced Roast Beef Sandwiches

**Wheat bread**

**1 to 1 1/2 lb. shaved beef, precooked**

**Toppings: pickles, lettuce, mayonnaise**

1. Make sandwiches.
2. Serve hot or cold.
3. Add desired toppings.

## Macaroni and Cabbage Salad

**8 oz. pinwheel macaroni**
**1/2 c. mayonnaise**
**1/4 c. sugar**
**1 T. vinegar**
**1 tsp. celery salt**
**1 tsp. Mrs. Dash**

**3 oz. Cheddar cheese, cubed**
**1/2 c. cabbage, chopped**
**1/4 c. onion, chopped**
**Salt & pepper to taste**

1. Boil 1 cup macaroni until tender; drain.
2. Rinse with cold water; drain.
3. In separate bowl, mix mayonnaise and sugar.
4. Then add vinegar and seasonings.
5. Now add prepared sauce to macaroni.
6. Add chopped cabbage, onions, and cheese in small cubes.
7. Refrigerate.

## Prepare for Week 12:
1.   Defrost rolled rump roast.
2.   Marinate overnight in covered plastic container.
3.   Chill fruit cocktail.

# Notes & Recipes

# SEASONING GUIDE

Get acquainted with spices and herbs. Add in small amounts, 1/4 teaspoon for each 4 servings. Taste before adding more. Crush dried herbs or snip fresh herbs before using. If substituting fresh for dried, use 3 times more fresh herbs.

### Appetizers, Soups

**STUFFED CELERY:** Mix caraway seed with cream cheese; fill celery. Dash with paprika.

**TOMATO COCKTAIL:** Add 1/4 teaspoon dried basil per cup.

**CHICKEN SOUP:** Add a dash of rosemary, tarragon, or nutmeg. Sprinkle paprika atop for color.

**CLAM CHOWDER:** Add a dash of caraway seed, sage, or thyme.

**CONSOMMÉ:** Dash in basil, marjoram, savory, or tarragon.

**MUSHROOM SOUP:** Season with curry, oregano, or marjoram.

**ONION SOUP:** Add marjoram.

**OYSTER STEW:** Lightly add cayenne, mace, or marjoram.

**POTATO SOUP:** Dash with mustard or basil. Top with snipped chives or parsley.

**SPLIT-PEA SOUP:** Add dash basil, chili powder, or rosemary.

**TOMATO SOUP:** Dash in basil, dill, oregano, sage, or tarragon.

**VEGETABLE SOUP:** Try allspice, oregano, sage, or thyme.

### Breads, Pasta

**BISCUITS:** Add caraway seed, thyme, or savory to flour. Serve with meat.

**BREAD:** Make each loaf a surprise by adding caraway seed, cardamom, or poppy seed.

**COFFEE CAKE:** Mix crushed anise in batter. For variety, sprinkle cinnamon-sugar mixture atop or add poppy seed filling.

**CORNBREAD:** Add poultry seasoning or caraway seed to dry ingredients. Be adventuresome; add 1/2 teaspoon rosemary to batter.

**CROUTONS:** Toss toast cubes in melted butter seasoned with basil, marjoram, or onion salt.

**DOUGHNUTS:** Add mace or nutmeg to dry ingredients. After frying, roll in cinnamon-sugar.

**DUMPLINGS:** Add thyme or parsley (fresh or flakes) to batter.

**MUFFINS:** Blueberry -- add dash of nutmeg to dry ingredients. Season plain muffins with caraway or cinnamon.

**NOODLES:** Butter, then sprinkle with poppy seed.

**ROLLS:** Add caraway seed. Or, sprinkle with sesame seed.

**SPAGHETTI:** Toss with butter, Parmesan, and snipped chives.

### Eggs, Cheese

**BAKED EGGS:** Sprinkle dash of thyme or paprika over the top.

**CREAMED EGGS:** Add mace.

**DEVILED EGGS:** Add celery seed, cumin, mustard, savory, chili powder, or curry powder.

**OMELET:** Try with dash of marjoram or rosemary (go easy!).

**SCRAMBLED EGGS:** Sprinkle lightly with basil, thyme, rosemary, or marjoram. Add seasoning near the end of cooking.

**SOUFFLÉ:** Add 1/4 teaspoon marjoram to 4-egg soufflé. To cheese soufflé, add basil or savory.

**CHEESE CASSEROLES:** Spark with dash sage or marjoram.

**CHEESE FONDUE:** Try adding a dash of basil or nutmeg.

**CHEESE RAREBIT:** Try with mace or mustard.

**CHEESE SAUCE:** Add mustard or a dash of marjoram or thyme.

**CHEESE SPREAD:** Blend sage, caraway seed, thyme, or celery seed into melted processed cheese.

**COTTAGE CHEESE:** Blend in chives or a dash of sage, caraway seed, dill, anise or cumin. Prepare several hours ahead of time.

# Week Twelve

**Day 1**  Beef Rolled Rump Roast
Roasted Vegetables
Wild Rice Casserole
Fruit Cocktail

**Day 2**  Bratwurst Sandwiches
Sauerkraut
Potato Chips
Apple Wedges

**Day 3**  Barbecue Beef Sandwiches
Creamy Hashbrowns
Grapes

**Day 4**  Tuna Casserole
Peas
Red Gelatin Delight

**Day 5**  London Broil
Cabbage and Ham Slaw
Pineapple and Bananas

**Day 6**  Meatloaf
Creamed Corn
Mashed Potatoes
Orange Slices

**Week 12:** Beef Roast, Bratwurst, BBQ Beef,
Tuna Casserole, London Broil, Meat Loaf

## Bakery
hot dog buns
hamburger buns

## Baking Goods
(sugar)
(flour, salt, pepper)
(garlic powder, sage)
dry mustard, brown sugar
3 oz. red gelatin
4 oz. walnuts, chopped

## Dairy
milk, butter, eggs
8 oz. sour cream
pint half & half
4 oz. shredded Cheddar cheese
16 oz. Velveeta cheese

## Frozen Foods
10 oz. peas
2 lb. hashbrowns
8 oz. whipped topping

## Produce
5 lb. potatoes
4 onions, celery, carrots
cabbage, radishes
green pepper
3 apples, 3 oranges
3 bananas, grapes

## Packaged Goods
(ketchup)
(mustard, oil, vinegar)
(lemon juice)
(teriyaki and soy sauce)
barbecue sauce
Worcestershire sauce
dry, fine bread crumbs
24 oz. creamed corn
24 oz. sauerkraut
6 oz. mushrooms
16 oz. crushed pineapple
17 oz. pineapple chunks
10 oz. potato soup
10 oz. cream of mushroom soup
2 cans cream of celery soup
2 (7 oz.) cans tuna
box instant wild rice
box instant brown rice
(instant mashed potatoes)
8 oz. wide noodles
potato chips

## Meat
4 to 8 bratwurst
4 to 6 London broils
4 lb. rump roast
1 1/2 lb. ground beef
1 lb. buffet ham, precooked

# Day 1

## Beef Rolled Rump Roast

4 to 6 lb. rolled rump roast
    (same directions for
    cooking as pork roast,
    Week 9, Day 1; except
    cooking time 1 3/4 to
    2 1/2 hours)
    (save extra beef for Day 3)

## Roasted Vegetables

8 potatoes, peeled &
    quartered

6 carrots, scraped & sliced
    in half lengthwise
1 onion, quartered

## Wild Rice Casserole

1 c. wild rice (Uncle Ben's)
1/2 c. quick brown rice

4 slices Velveeta cheese
1 (3 oz.) can mushrooms

Sauté:
1/2 c. onions, chopped
1/2 c. celery, chopped

1/4 c. butter

1/4 c. Half & Half cream

1. Cook rice according to box instructions with 2 cups water.
2. Sauté onions and celery with butter.
3. Mix all ingredients in 3-quart low casserole dish.
4. Pour cream on top.
5. Bake at 350° for 1 hour.

## Chilled Fruit Cocktail

# Day 2

## Bratwurst Sandwiches

**4 to 8 bratwurst sausages**       **Mustard**
**Hot dog buns**                    **Chopped onions**

1. Fry bratwurst in skillet with 1/2 cup water.
2. Use splatter screen.
3. Turn several times, browning both sides.
4. Add more water if needed. (Some people use beer.)

## Sauerkraut

**1 (24 oz.) can/jar sauerkraut**

1. Heat in saucepan on stove.
2. Serve in sandwich or on the side.

## Potato Chips

## Apple Wedges

# Day 3

## Barbecue Beef Sandwiches

**(See Day 1)**

**Cooked beef roast,
  shredded**
**1/2 c. onions, diced**

**2 T. oil**
**1 c. barbecue sauce**
**Hamburger buns**

1. Brown beef roast and onions with oil in pan.
2. Add barbecue sauce.
3. Simmer for at least 30 minutes.
4. Add water and more sauce for longer cooking time.
5. Serve hot in hamburger buns.

## Creamy Hash Browns

**SAUCE:**
**4 oz. sour cream**
**5 oz. cream of potato soup**
**5 oz. cream of celery soup**

**1/2 c. milk**
**1/4 c. shredded Cheddar
  cheese**

**1 lb. frozen hash browns,
  thawed**

1. Use a 7x11-inch baking dish.
2. Pour in hash browns.
3. Mix remaining ingredients together.
4. Pour over hash browns.
5. Bake at 350° for 30 to 35 minutes.

## Grapes

**Prepare For Day 4:**
1. Make Red Gelatin Delight.

# Day 4

## Tuna Noodle Casserole

2 (7 oz.) cans tuna
1 (10 oz.) can cream of
    mushroom soup

1 (10 oz.) can cream of
    celery soup
1 (10 oz.) can milk

8 oz. wide egg noodles

1. Boil water in medium saucepan.
2. Add noodles and cook 10 minutes until tender.
3. Drain.
4. Combine remaining ingredients in casserole dish.
5. Cover.
6. Microwave for 5 minutes on HIGH.
7. Stir.
8. Add noodles and microwave for 4 minutes, or until cooked through.

## Green Peas

10 oz. frozen peas

1. Simmer on stove with 1/4 cup water in medium-size covered saucepan for 5 minutes.
   (Best if bright green color.)

## Red Gelatin Delight

3 oz. red gelatin
1 c. boiling water
1/2 c. pineapple juice
8 oz. non-dairy whipped
    topping

2 oz. chopped nuts
1 (8 oz.) can crushed
    pineapple, drained

1. Prepare gelatin and cool until thickened, <u>not set</u>!
2. Fold in remaining ingredients.
3. Refrigerate in serving bowl.
4. Let set.

## Prepare for Day 5:

1. Defrost London Broils.
2. Marinate overnight.
3. Defrost buffet ham.
4. Make Cabbage and Ham Slaw.
5. Chill pineapple chunks.

# Day 5

## London Broil

**(See Day 4 for directions)**

**4 to 6 London Broils, wrapped
    in bacon (premade in meat
    department)**

**MARINADE:**
**1/4 c. teriyaki sauce**

**2 T. soy sauce**
**Garlic powder**

1.  Marinate meat at least 1 hour.
2.  Grill or broil meat until desired doneness.

## Cabbage and Ham Slaw

**2 c. cubed, buffet ham**

**EGG MIXTURE:**
**2 egg yolks, beaten**

**3 T. vinegar**
**2 T. lemon juice**

**THICKENING:**
**2 T. flour**
**2 T. sugar**

**1 tsp. salt**
**1 tsp. dry mustard**
**1 c. milk**

**VEGETABLES:**
**4 to 6 cabbage leaves**
**4 c. cabbage, shredded**

**1 sm. onion, chopped**
**1/2 green pepper, chopped**
**6 radishes, sliced**

1.  Mix dry thickening ingredients.
2.  Gradually add milk, stirring well until smooth. (Can shake in pint jar with lid.)
3.  Cook on low heat, stirring constantly until thick.
4.  Combine egg mixture ingredients in medium bowl.
5.  Slowly add thickened to egg mixture.
6.  Then pour all back into pan and heat on low for 1 minute; cool.
7.  Toss vegetables with cubed ham.
8.  Mix cooled mixed sauce in with vegetables and ham.
9.  Serve over individual cabbage leaf.

# Pineapple and Bananas

**17 oz. pineapple chunks**          **2 bananas, sliced**

1.  Combine pineapple chunks and bananas.
2.  Serve in individual cups.

## Prepare for Day 6:
1.  Thaw ground beef.

# Day 6

## Meatloaf

2 eggs, beaten
1/4 c. milk
1 1/2 lb. ground beef

1/2 c. fine, dry bread
    crumbs

SEASONINGS:
1/4 c. med. onion, diced
1 tsp. salt

1/2 tsp. sage
1/8 tsp. pepper

SAUCE:
2/3 c. ketchup
1 T. brown sugar

1 T. prepared mustard
1 T. lemon juice
1 T. Worcestershire sauce

1.  In large bowl, mix eggs and milk.
2.  Stir in onion, salt, sage and pepper.
3.  Add ground beef and bread crumbs; mix well.
4.  Use bread loaf pan.
5.  Shape meat and bake at 375° for 1 hour; drain.

**Sauce:**
6.  Mix ingredients and microwave in covered salad bowl for 1 minute.
7.  Spread on meatloaf.
8.  Bake for 10 minutes.

## Mashed Potatoes

1 box instant potatoes

1.  Prepare according to box directions.

## Creamed Corn

17 to 24 oz. can creamed corn

1.  Microwave in medium-size covered bowl for 4 minutes.

## Orange Slices

## Prepare for Week 1:
1.  Thaw chicken in cold water.
2.  Refrigerate when thawed.

# Notes & Recipes

# Caloric Values

Abbreviations: av. = average, c. = cup, lg. = large, med. = medium, pc. = piece, sl. = slice, sm. = small, sq. = square, sv. = serving, t. = teaspoon, T. = tablespoon.

**Calories**          **Calories**

**Meats**

Beef

| | |
|---|---|
| Hamburger, 1 cake | 100 |
| Roast, lean, av. sl. | 100 |
| Steak, av. sl. | 100 |

Poultry

| | |
|---|---|
| Broiled chicken, 1/2 | 100 |
| Fried chicken, 5 oz. | 310 |
| Roasted chicken, 5 oz. | 270 |
| Turkey, dark, w/o skin | 260 |
| Turkey, light, w/o skin | 220 |
| Turkey, 1 sl. | 100 |

Pork

| | |
|---|---|
| Bacon, 4 strips | 100 |
| Chop, broiled | 200 |
| Ham, baked, 4x4x1/8" | 100 |
| Roast, 1 sl. | 170 |
| Sausage, link, 2 med. | 100 |
| Spareribs, 4 ribs | 150 |
| Tenderloin, 1 pc. | 200 |

**Seafood**

| | |
|---|---|
| Codfish cakes, 2 lg. | 200 |
| Crabmeat, canned, 1/2 c. | 75 |
| Haddock, av. sl. | 100 |
| Halibut, 1 pc. | 100 |
| Perch, 1 med. | 95 |
| Scallops, 6 | 100 |
| Shrimp, 10 | 50 |
| Shrimp cocktail, 1/2 c. | 100 |
| Tuna, canned, 1/2 c. | 100 |

**Vegetables**

| | |
|---|---|
| Asparagus, canned, 1/2 c. | 20 |
| Asparagus, 6 fr. stalks | 15 |
| Beans, baked, 2/3 c. | 200 |
| Beans, lima, 1/2 c. | 100 |
| Beans, navy, 1/2 c. | 160 |
| Beans, string, 1/2 c. | 25 |
| Beets, 2 med. | 45 |
| Broccoli, 1/2 c. | 20 |
| Brussels sprouts, 6 | 50 |
| Cabbage, cooked, 3/4 c. | 20 |
| Cabbage, raw, 1/2 c. | 15 |
| Carrots, cooked, 1/2 c. | 30 |
| Carrots, raw, 4 med. | 20 |

**Vegetables** (Continued)

| | |
|---|---|
| Cauliflower, 1 c. | 30 |
| Celery, 3 stalks | 10 |
| Corn, canned, 1/2 c. | 100 |
| Corn on cob, 1 lg. ear | 100 |
| Cucumber, 12 sl. | 10 |
| Lettuce, 1/4 head | 15 |
| Okra, 1 c. | 30 |
| Onions, cooked, 1/2 c. | 40 |
| Onions, green, 5 sm. | 10 |
| Peas, canned, 1/2 c. | 55 |
| Peas, fresh, 1/2 c. | 75 |
| Peppers, 2 sm. | 25 |
| Potato, baked, 1 med. | 100 |
| Potato, boiled, 2 sm. | 100 |
| Potato, mashed, 1/2 c. | 100 |
| Potato, sweet, 1/2 lg. | 150 |
| Radishes, 5 | 15 |
| Sauerkraut, 2/3 c. | 25 |
| Spinach, 3/4 c. | 25 |
| Tomato, canned, 1 c. | 50 |
| Tomato, fresh, 1 sm. | 25 |
| Tomato juice, 1/2 c. | 25 |

**Fruits**

| | |
|---|---|
| Apple, raw, 1 lg. | 100 |
| Applesauce, 1/2 c. | 150 |
| Apricots, canned, 6 | 150 |
| Apricots, fresh, 3 | 60 |
| Banana, 2 med. | 100 |
| Berries, fresh, 1/2 c. | 50 |
| Cantaloupe, 1/2 | 50 |
| Cherries, canned, 1/2 c. | 100 |
| Grapefruit, 1/2 | 50 |
| Grapefruit juice, 1/3 c. | 70 |
| Grape juice, 1/2 c. | 100 |
| Grapes, 20-25 | 75 |
| Honeydew Melon, 1/4 | 100 |
| Lemon juice, 3 T. | 15 |
| Orange, 1 | 70 |
| Orange juice, 1/2 c. | 50 |
| Peaches, canned, 2 | 100 |
| Peaches, fresh, 1 med. | 50 |
| Pears, canned, 3 | 100 |
| Pears, fresh, 2 med. | 95 |
| Pineapple, canned, 1 sl. | 100 |

# Caloric Values (continued)

|  | **Calories** |  | **Calories** |
|---|---|---|---|

**Fruits** (Continued)

Pineapple, fresh, 1/2 c. ...................... 60
Pineapple juice, 1/2 c. ...................... 75
Rhubarb, stewed, 1/2 c. .................. 100
Tangerine, 1 ...................................... 35
Watermelon, 1 sl., 1/4" .................. 100

**Cheese & Eggs**

Cheese, Amer., 1 cube ...................... 80
Cheese, cottage, 1/4 c. ...................... 60
Cheese, Swiss, 1/8" sl. .................... 100
Eggs, fried, 1 .................................... 120
Eggs, 1 whole .................................... 70
Eggs, scrambled, 1/4 c. .................. 100

**Breads**

Biscuits, 2 sm. .................................. 100
Coffeecake, 1 1/2" sq. ...................... 100
Corn, 2"x2"x1" sq. .......................... 100
Cracker, Graham, 1 .......................... 35
Cracker, saltine, 1 ............................ 15
Melba toast, 1 sl. .............................. 25
Muffin, 1 sm. .................................... 135
Pancake, 1 ........................................ 60
Pretzel, 5 sticks ................................ 18
Raisin, 1 sl. ...................................... 100
Roll, sweet, 1 .................................... 175
Rye, 1 sl. .......................................... 65
Waffle, 1 ............................................ 215
White, 1 sl. ........................................ 65
Whole wheat, 1 sl. ............................ 75
Zwieback, 1 ...................................... 20

**Cereals**

Bran flakes, 2/3 c. ............................ 100
Corn flakes, 1 c. ................................ 100
Cream of Wheat ................................ 75
Oatmeal, 1/2 c. .................................. 80
Puffed Rice, 1 c. ................................ 60

**Desserts & Sweets**

Angel food cake, med. sl. ................ 150
Corn syrup, 1 T. ................................ 85
Doughnut, plain, 1 ............................ 120
Honey, 1 T. ...................................... 100
Ice cream, plain 1/2 c. ...................... 200
Jello, 1 c. .......................................... 75
Jelly, 1 T. .......................................... 65
Marshmallows, 5 .............................. 100
Plain cookie, 1 .................................. 50
Sugar, brown, 2 t. ............................ 35
Sugar, plain, 2 t. .............................. 50

**Beverages**

Cocoa, with milk, 1 c. ...................... 180
Coffee, black, 1 c. ............................ 0
Coffee, 1 T. cream, 1 c. .................... 50
Ginger ale, 1 c. ................................ 75
Lemonade, 1 c. .................................. 100
Milk, skim, 1 c. ................................ 90
Milk, whole, 1 c. .............................. 170
Tea .................................................... 0

**Miscellaneous**

Butter, 1" sq. .................................... 80
Catsup, 1 T. ...................................... 25
French dressing, 1 T. ........................ 75
Gravy, thick, 3 T. .............................. 100
Macaroni, 1/2 c. ................................ 90
Margarine, 1 T. ................................ 100
Mayonnaise, 1 T. .............................. 100
Olive oil, 1 T. .................................... 100
Peanut butter, 1 T. ............................ 100
Pecans, 6 halves .............................. 50
Pickles, 1/2 c. .................................... 25
Popcorn, plain, 1 c. .......................... 55
Potato chips, 9 .................................. 100
Spaghetti, 3/4 c. ................................ 100

# Index

*Each recipe title is followed by the week and day (in parentheses) the recipe appears.*

## MEAT

## SANDWICHES



## SOUPS



## VEGETABLES

### Asparagus



### Beans



### Broccoli



### Brussels Sprouts



### Cabbage

### Grapes



### Melons



### Oranges



### Peaches



### Pears



### Pineapple



### Strawberries



### Miscellaneous

# Notes & Recipes

**ORDER BLANK**

NAME _______________________________________________

ADDRESS_____________________________________________

CITY & STATE ______________________________  ZIP __________

How many copies? ____________  Amount enclosed ___________
    Price per book............................ $12.00
    Tax (Iowa 5%)................................... .60
    Postage & handling..........................2.00
    Total ....................................... $14.60
Please make checks payable to: THE KITCHEN CUPBOARD
       Mail orders to:  The Kitchen Cupboard      Item No. 55
                    P.O. Box 106
Ph. 515-448-5747        Clarion, IA 50525      1-800-494-0305

---

**ORDER BLANK**

NAME _______________________________________________

ADDRESS_____________________________________________

CITY & STATE ______________________________  ZIP __________

How many copies? ____________  Amount enclosed ___________
    Price per book............................ $12.00
    Tax (Iowa 5%)................................... .60
    Postage & handling..........................2.00
    Total ....................................... $14.60
Please make checks payable to: THE KITCHEN CUPBOARD
       Mail orders to:  The Kitchen Cupboard      Item No. 55
                    P.O. Box 106
Ph. 515-448-5747        Clarion, IA 50525      1-800-494-0305



---

**ORDER BLANK**

NAME _______________________________________________

ADDRESS_____________________________________________

CITY & STATE ______________________________  ZIP __________

How many copies? ____________  Amount enclosed ___________
    Price per book............................ $12.00
    Tax (Iowa 5%)................................... .60
    Postage & handling..........................2.00
    Total ....................................... $14.60
Please make checks payable to: THE KITCHEN CUPBOARD
       Mail orders to:  The Kitchen Cupboard      Item No. 55
                    P.O. Box 106
Ph. 515-448-5747        Clarion, IA 50525      1-800-494-0305

# EXCELLENT FUNDRAISING IDEAS

In addition to printing cookbooks for fund raising organizations, JUMBO JACK'S COOKBOOKS also offers the proven successful fund raising products shown below. The products shown below are just a few of the many items you might select for your next fund raising project, or perhaps in conjunction with your cookbook project. Any of these will be beautifully imprinted with your organization's logo and name.

If you are interested in helping your organization make money with these successful fund raising products, just mark the products you'd like more information about, give us your name and address.

Name —

Address—

Tear out this page and mail it to:  **JUMBO JACK'S COOKBOOKS**
**301 Broadway • P.O. Box 247 • Audubon, Iowa 50025**

Or if you prefer, give Mike, Mitzi or Jeanne a toll free call at 1-800-798-2635
FAX 1-712-563-3118     COLLECT: 1-712-563-2635

We hope you are enjoying using this cookbook and find it useful in your kitchen. This book was printed by Jumbo Jack's Cookbooks. If you are interested in having cookbooks printed for your organization, please write us for prices and details.

A cookbook is a good way for YOUR organization to make money.

If you are interested in more information, just tear out this page and mail it to us with your name and address, or just call us toll-free 1-800-798-2635.

## Featuring the 3-ring easel binder

We also do hardback covers, square back wire covers, and other types of binding

Yes — please send me more information

Name _______________________________________________

Organization _________________________________________

Address _____________________________________________

City ________________ State ________ Zip ____________

Phone ______________________________________________

**UP TO 5 MONTHS INTEREST FREE!**

Or, if you prefer give Mike, Mitzi or Jeanne a call:
Toll free: 1-800-798-2635; Collect: 1-712-563-2635
FAX: 1-712-563-3118